In *Rapture: Delayed?*, Craig [...] church. Whatever your theo[...] you will appreciate the way he systematically, analytically, and passionately presents the information. *Rapture: Delayed?* will cause you to affirm or rethink your position through the light of God's Word. It's obvious this was a labor of love, and you will thoroughly enjoy this book—whether for review, research, or recreational reading.

ROCKY A. BARRA, LEAD PASTOR
CONNECTION CHURCH, CANTON, MI

The message of *Rapture: Delayed?* relies solely on the Holy Scriptures. Craig has done his studies on the subject of the rapture of the Church, and I believe he has uncovered the truth. His desire to share this truth and, thereby, prepare the Church is clearly the goal of this well-documented and well-written book.

JOYCE MURCH, FEATURES EDITOR
INTERNATIONAL DOLL ARTIST MAGAZINE;
OWNER, JOYCE MURCH DOLL COMPANY

Rapture: Delayed?

RAPTURE: DELAYED?

CRAIG PLANTS

Rapture: Delayed?
Copyright © 2013 by Craig Plants

All rights reserved. No part of this book may be reproduced or transmitted in any form or by any means, electronic or mechanical, including photocopying and recording, or by any information storage and retrieval system, without permission in writing from the publisher.

Scripture quotations are taken from The King James Version

DEEP RIVER BOOKS
Sisters, Oregon
www.deepriverbooks.com

ISBN-13: 9781937756741
ISBN-10: 1937756745

Library of Congress: 201295513

Cover Design by Jason Enterline

Dedication

My parents, who introduced me to light and life in Christ.

The late Mason Murch, my mentor and my friend.
I look forward to seeing him again.

Terry Scott Taylor, whose lyrics and music have challenged me and
expanded my knowledge of God.

Greg "Manchild" Owens.

"Take, my brethren, the prophets, who
have spoken in the name of the Lord, for an example of
suffering affliction, and of patience.
Behold, we count them happy which endure.
Ye have heard of the patience of Job, and have seen
the end of the Lord; that the Lord is very pitiful, and of tender mercy."

JAMES 5:10–11

Table of Contents

INTRODUCTION:	How It All Began	11
CHAPTER 1:	A Brief History of the Pretribulation Rapture Doctrine	15
CHAPTER 2:	What Are the Signs of His Coming? A Chronological Step-by-Step Answer	33
CHAPTER 3:	The First Warning: Take Heed, Pay Attention, Do Not Be Deceived	37
CHAPTER 4:	The First Three Signs: Deception, War, and the Beginning of Sorrows	41
CHAPTER 5:	The Fourth Sign: Worldwide Gospel Witness	53
CHAPTER 6:	The Fifth Sign: Persecution	57
CHAPTER 7:	The Sixth Sign: The Antichrist Is Proclaimed God and the Strong Delusion	71
CHAPTER 8:	The Jews and the Mark of the Beast	87
CHAPTER 9:	The Seven, Eighth, and Ninth Signs: Great Tribulation, False Christs, Heaven and Earth Shaken	97
CHAPTER 10:	The Tenth Sign: The Mystery of God Revealed at the Last Trump—The Return of Jesus Christ	107
CHAPTER 11:	The Final Warnings of Jesus	119
CHAPTER 12:	The Wrath of God	133
CHAPTER 13:	Children of the Great Tribulation	141
CHAPTER 14:	The Salvation of God: Come One, Come All	159
INDEX:	Summary of The Signs	173
ENDNOTES		187

INTRODUCTION
How It All Began

The Bible talks a great deal about mystery. The King James Bible uses the word twenty-two times. But what I find especially interesting about the word *mystery* in the Bible is that it's never used to hide or conceal a truth. Rather, each time the word is used, a truth of God is revealed. As Jesus said to his disciples in Mark 4:11, "Unto you it is given to know the mystery of the kingdom of God: but unto them that are without, all these things are done in parables."

Within the evangelical church today, many teach that the rapture of the church by Jesus Christ, which will happen before the start of the Great Tribulation, is a mystery that will spring upon us without warning at any moment. Churches that believe this rarely teach or acknowledge any other view. For years, I never questioned the validity of this teaching. I believed, like many other Christians, that the return of Christ was imminent and that we could be raptured away at any time. I had no reason to doubt this teaching, since it was prevalent in the various Bible and Baptist churches I have attended throughout my life. However, my closely held pretribulation rapture belief system all changed when I took a fresh and unencumbered look at what the Scripture teaches regarding the return of Christ.

Where It All Started

During a Sunday morning church service in March 2010, it occurred to me that the doctrine of the pretribulation rapture did not have a solid scriptural basis. It started with a church survey asking for suggestions on topics of study. I responded with "rapture doctrine."

I had good reason for wanting to undertake such a study. I had been in church my entire life, with nearly forty years of the church's teaching under my belt. Yet that Sunday morning, I realized that I could not explain, using Scripture, why I believed that the rapture of the church would happen before the Great Tribulation. Despite my faithful church attendance, I could not provide a single Scripture reference or context to explain the doctrine of the pretribulation rapture. I thought this was curious, especially since the doctrine had been forcefully taught by many pastors and teachers over the years. In some evangelical circles, the doctrine of the pretribulation rapture seems to have been settled without debate and with very little Scripture to prove it.

In addition to my church attendance, I have explored the Bible on my own. On the Sunday morning of the survey, I was on my twenty-ninth reading of the Bible in three years and three months, an average of one read-through every forty days and my thirty-ninth reading overall. My Bible of choice is the King James Version of *The Reese Chronological Bible,* which organizes the Bible into chronological events as they happened in history (I highly recommend reading the Bible this way). I also had been teaching young adult and adult Sunday school for more than fifteen years. However, even with all my self-study and teaching, I could not explain why I believed what I believed about the end.

When I was honest with myself, it seemed my main reason for believing the pretribulation rapture doctrine was because it had been taught with such authority by so many. In other words, someone had told me what to believe. And I had never questioned it.

As the sermon that Sunday began, the preacher turned to 1 Corinthians 15:51–52:

> Behold, I shew you a mystery; we shall not all sleep, but we shall all be changed, in a moment, in the twinkling of an eye, at the last trump: for the trumpet shall sound, and the dead shall be raised incorruptible, and we shall be changed.

The very same morning that I began to question my understanding of the Rapture, the sermon touched briefly on the Rapture. Coincidence? Or divine providence? It's hard to prove either way, but what I can tell you is this: From that point forward, beginning right there in the pew, I began to search the Scriptures in a whole new way.

My desire to discover now became a pressing need to share. A salesman by trade, I decided a PowerPoint overview of my findings would be a good start. After all, everyone loves a PowerPoint, right? In the end, I had prepared a sixty-seven-page presentation.

From that point, I shared the information with my wife, a business associate, friends, parents, a deacon, and a seasoned Baptist preacher. None of them could expose flaws in what I had prepared. The deacon, Mason Murch, concluded our four-hour discussion by saying, "This is Scripture; you cannot dispute it." The Baptist minister simply stated, "You have given me a lot to think about."

Why You Should Read This Book

After much consideration, I decided to turn the PowerPoint into a document that could be read and shared among the wider church body, one that explains a mystery—a difficult topic—in simple terms that can be easily remembered. This book is the result of that decision.

In the pages to come, I have assembled the majority of the Scriptures that deal with the end times in a format that shows how they complement each other in support of a rapture that takes place *during* the great tribulation period, not before it. Once you see how these puzzle pieces assemble into a complete picture, I believe you will find it difficult to disassemble them and try to make these same Scriptures support a pre-, exact mid-, or post-tribulation rapture viewpoint.

My goal is for people of all denominations to take a fresh look at their beliefs about the end times and consider the implications if their current beliefs turn out to be wrong. The Bible warns us multiple times to be on guard against all manner of deception regarding the return of Christ. This clearly implies that there will be deception in end-time teachings, and we must be willing to step back and review our own beliefs in order to be on guard against it.

My hope is that Christians everywhere will base their beliefs solely on the Bible and reject the false teachings of man. Please don't believe things about the Bible or about God just because someone told you they were true. Find out for yourself by studying on your own. As history draws to a close, the true doctrine of the rapture is paramount to the health of the church during the end times. Without a correct understanding of the end times, believers may become confused as they try to match their doctrine to current events, or they may ignore Scripture's light on their circumstances altogether. They will be open to the end-time deception that Jesus plainly and frequently warned us about.

Given the profound implications of the raging deception that will accompany the end times, I will start with this plea:

Are you willing to take a fresh look at the Word of God, pray, and seek his counsel in these matters of great consequence?

Chapter 1

A Brief History of the Pretribulation Rapture Doctrine

The Rapture of the saints by Jesus Christ—the time when Jesus will return for his people and take them away to heaven in a moment of time. Talk about a hot topic! People of all walks of life are drawn to end-times discussion, whether within the church or without. As this book goes to publication, we are in the last days of 2012, the year when many predict the world will end. There are reports of people building shelters in the desert in preparation. I recently watched a show on people called "preppers," who are stockpiling supplies for coming trouble. The *Left Behind* series has sold millions. Fundamentalist preachers proclaim that Jesus' return is imminent.

Given the events in the world around us, it is no wonder that so many care so much about this topic. As our perception grows that natural disasters, economic chaos, cultural upheaval, and political events appear to be accelerating toward a crescendo, the church's teaching regarding the return of Christ is becoming a central focus of our belief system.

Authoritative Teaching?

The pretribulation rapture is a doctrine about which many people feel strongly and preach authoritatively. But is their teaching truly authoritative? When the question of the end times and the timing of the Rapture was first impressed upon me that Sunday morning in 2010, I started researching the Bible for myself without the aid of a study guide or commentary. I wanted to understand what the Scripture—the only *real* authority—said before I became influenced by the writings of others.

Through experience, I have learned that God can teach me to understand his Bible. After I came to understand God's ability to teach me his Word directly, I discovered another man who had the same experience.

George Müller (1805–1898) was an evangelist and the director of the Ashley Down Orphanage in Bristol, England, where he cared for more than ten thousand orphans in his lifetime. He wrote:

> That the word of God alone is our standard of judgment in spiritual things; that it can be explained only by the Holy Spirit; and that in our day, as well as in former times, he is the teacher of his people. And, further, that the Holy Spirit alone can teach us about our state by nature, show us the need of a Saviour, enable us to believe in Christ, explain to us the Scriptures, help us in preaching, etc. It was my beginning to understand this latter point in particular which had a great effect on me; *for the Lord enabled me to put it to the test of experience, by laying aside commentaries, and almost every other book, and simply reading the word of God and studying it.* The result of this was, that the first evening that I shut myself into my room, to give myself to prayer and meditation over the Scriptures, *I learned more in a few hours than I had done during a period of several months previously.* (emphasis mine)[1]

For many years, just like George Müller, I have used the Bible as my main text for learning about God. When I began to think and study in earnest about the coming of Christ, it wasn't long before all the pieces regarding the Rapture fell into place of their own accord. The end result is the book you now read.

After the first draft of this book was completed, I began to research the subject to determine how my writing compared to other viewpoints. What I found surprised me. While I had experienced the sincere preaching of many pretribulation proponents, I had no idea that people were so adamant in their beliefs regarding the end times and the timing of the Rapture!

One pretribulation enthusiast on the Web went as far as to call any other rapture doctrine an abomination and blasphemy, as well as cynical and church-hating. There were so many putdowns in his writing that I had to look up some of the words! However, I don't consider myself cynical or church-hating. Rather, my goal is to have people consider what the Bible says in its entirety and make informed decisions on the facts presented by *the most authoritative source we have*—the Word of God. I do not believe that I need to convince you of the truth. If this book contains the truth of the Word of God, then it will be convincing on its own.

A Brief History of the Rapture

Before we begin our study through the Bible, let's take a moment to review the history of the rapture doctrine. The doctrines can be roughly categorized into four areas:

- Pretribulation: Advocates the Rapture at the beginning of the seven-year tribulation period.
- Midtribulation: Advocates the Rapture at the exact middle of the seven-year tribulation period—three-and-a-half years from the start.
- Prewrath: Advocates the Rapture before the start of the vial judgments that contain the Wrath of God (Rev. 16:1).
- Post-tribulation: Advocates the Rapture at the end of the Great Tribulation.

Not long into my research, I discovered that there is a debate regarding the origins of the pretribulation rapture doctrine. Some claim that the doctrine was born in the 1830s, while others claim it was mentioned in the fourth century in writings by Pseudo-Ephraem, an otherwise unknown writer. (It was common practice during the fourth century for unknown writers to create works using the name of someone who was well respected.) The sermon contained fifteen hundred words on three themes, "On the Last Times, the Antichrist, and the End of the World," which are presented in a chronological fashion. It is believed that this sermon was widely circulated among orthodox circles of the day.

What surprised me most is that after this one sermon in the fourth century, there is *no additional mention* of a pretribulation rapture doctrine in church history or writing for *centuries*. The concept does not show up again until the nineteenth century, in 1830. In fact, Scotland is the place where many believe that the pretribulation rapture doctrine truly originated. The story centers around a fifteen-year-old girl named Margaret MacDonald, who was involved in the Pentecostal movement. Margaret was considered a prophetess and is claimed to have had a vision that stated that Christians were to be raptured just prior to the Great Tribulation.[2]

Opponents to the pretribulation rapture often try to point to Margaret's vision as the questionable start of the doctrine, implying that it was of demonic origins. I'm not convinced that is a fair argument based on my reading of the written account of the vision: I must admit that I cannot identify where the pretribulation rapture is described or even alluded to in the writing!

A more sure and certain start for the doctrine can be traced to Edward Irving (1792–1834) of the Catholic Apostolic Church. Edward Irving is considered the forerunner of the Pentecostal and Charismatic movements.

Irving was driven by the notion that he was living in the last days and that he would see the return of Christ. In 1828, he wrote a book titled, *The Last Days: A Discourse on the Evil Character of These Our Times, Proving Them to be The 'Perilous Times' and the 'Last Days.'*

Here's what Edward Irving wrote in his first chapter:

> The times and fulness of the times, so often mentioned in the New Testament, I consider as referring to the great period numbered by times…Now if this reasoning be correct, as there can be little doubt that the one thousand two hundred and sixty days concluded in the year 1792, and the thirty additional days in the year 1823, we are already entered upon the last days, and the ordinary life of a man will carry many of us to the end of them. If this be so, it gives to the subject with which we have introduced this year's ministry a very great importance indeed.[3]

Obviously, Irving was wrong about the timing of the end, since his entire generation is now past. But his place in the history of the doctrine cannot be discounted on that basis. Within his sphere of influence is another key figure, John Nelson Darby (1800–1882) of the Plymouth Brethren.

John Nelson Darby was ordained an Anglican priest in 1826 and founded the Brethren in 1830. He began publishing his prophetic speculations in 1831.[4]

At nearly the same time, both Irving and Darby began to articulate two separate stages to Christ's return. This is the foundation of the pretribulation rapture doctrine as it is taught today. Irving and Darby speculated that there would be an invisible appearing of Christ when all Christians would be raptured from the earth, the Holy Spirit would be removed, the Antichrist would rise to power, and the seven-year tribulation period would begin. Only after this would Christ fully and visibly return to earth.

Darby became a huge proponent of the pretribulation rapture of the church. He was a church planter in Britain and Europe in the 1830s and 1840s, establishing Brethren churches and spreading his teaching regarding the end times. Darby gave a number of lectures which established his reputation as a leading interpreter of biblical prophecy and helped solidify the doctrine of a pretribulation rapture. He then made five missionary journeys to North America between 1862 and 1877, where he likewise spread his vision of the rapture of the church before the tribulation.

Leading theologians of the last few centuries commonly organized and spoke at conferences, to which pastors from all areas were invited to participate in discussions and lectures. Darby used a number of these conferences during his time in North America to spread his pretribulation rapture doctrine. This allowed him to influence a number of clergymen and laymen without the necessity of being part of their denomination.[5]

One of Darby's converts was James Hall Brookes, a Presbyterian pastor from St. Louis. From 1883 to 1897, Brookes led conferences each summer at Niagara-on-the-Lake, Ontario. The conferences were the breeding ground for the successful spread of the pretribulation rapture doctrine in America.

In 1897, a split divided the conference into two groups, a pro-Darby group and an anti-Darby group. What ensued was a five-year writing battle in which many doctrinal arguments were made. A key figure in the pro-Darby group was Cyrus Scofield. After five years, the debate had subsided, and the pro-Darby team continued to successfully spread their doctrine.

But the pretribulation rapture doctrine *really* took hold through the work of Cyrus Scofield. In 1903, Scofield started work on a reference Bible.

It took six years to complete, and it was published and promoted by Oxford University Press. The *Scofield Reference Bible*, which is still widely used today, uses the King James Version and includes extensive footnote commentaries by Cyrus Scofield and his consulting editors.

Within the *Scofield Reference Bible*, every passage relating to the end times provides commentary that cultivates the pretribulation rapture doctrine. By 1830, one million copies had been sold, which increased to two million copies by the end of 1945. This edition of the Bible has been heavily promoted, and its views have affected wide segments of the church. Its influence was not limited to the early twentieth century. Even though it was first published in 1909, the very first Bible my parents gave me in 1980 was the *Scofield Reference Bible*. To my recollection, nearly everyone in our church had one, and it was still heavily promoted well into the late 1980s (and beyond). While I was growing up, many of my church leaders and peers relied upon the references and cross-references that Scofield had documented to understand the Bible better. A natural result was an unquestioning belief in the pretribulation rapture doctrine within my circle of believers.

If you study the movement of the pretribulation doctrine, you'll discover that it first gained traction in the large cities of New York, Boston, Chicago, and St. Louis. From there, it spread to the West and to the South. Today, the doctrine is not taught in liberal Protestant denominations, but it is still strongly held and propagated in independent, nondenominational, full-gospel churches, and in many mainstream evangelical churches as well.

Perhaps surprisingly, the doctrine also is spread through American pop culture. Print media, radio, and TV all play their part. The media presents the doctrine with a mindset that takes for granted that the entire audience believes it unquestioningly. For example, the Rapture has been mentioned on *The Simpsons* (episode 354, May 8, 2005) and *American Dad*. In 1950, the novel *Raptured* by Ernest Angley focused on a man whose mother is raptured along with other Christians. Larry Norman wrote a popular song in 1969 titled, "I Wish We'd All Been Ready," about the surprise return of Christ. In the 1970s, Hal Lindsey wrote the popular book *The Late Great Planet Earth*, which tied the second coming of Christ to the rebirth of Israel.

I could bore you with a multitude of other examples (like the phenomenally successful *Left Behind* series), but I think you get the point. Between the pop culture of the last century and our current crop of Christian TV and radio programs, the doctrine of the pretribulation rapture is consistently referenced. Since its inception in the 1830s, this doctrine has snowballed into a ubiquitous pop culture idea.[6]

I suspect that many Christians would be surprised at this origin of the pretribulation doctrine, especially at how *new* it is in church history. I know I was. This doctrine is commonly taught in Pentecostal, Plymouth Brethren, Southern Baptist, and many other evangelical churches and is embraced by a large percentage of Christians today. However, given the brief and somewhat questionable history of the doctrine, I think it is fair to ask you to set aside your current-held beliefs for a moment and look at the Bible with a fresh pair of eyes. My hope is that the church will begin to debate and discuss the Rapture once again. The debate that raged at the turn of the twentieth century regarding the timing of the Rapture has died out—but this book is an attempt to revive it.

Critical Thinking: Rapture Doctrines and Consequences

When I first mentioned this topic to one of my friends, he said, "I don't think it matters." Chances are, he is voicing the opinion of many. *Why is the Rapture a matter of great consequence?* you ask.

I intend to show that the Rapture is a serious topic for the end-time believer—one that needs to be discussed logically, using Scripture references, with the implications and consequences of the competing doctrines in full view.

The remainder of this book will provide scriptural evidence for the rapture of the church at some point *after* the start of the Great Tribulation, and it will compare and contrast the pretribulation rapture to what I discovered in Scripture. Because I was taught the pretribulation rapture but then developed this book based on my own study of the Bible, I found myself needing a name for the doctrine I found in Scripture. The "great tribulation rapture" might not be the best moniker ever crafted, but it does succinctly describe what I now believe: that the Rapture will occur at an indeterminable point during the Great Tribulation.

At this point, I should distinguish between my belief and other post-tribulation positions. I do not advocate the Rapture at the *exact middle* of the Great Tribulation (midtribulation), nor do I advocate the Rapture at the end of the Great Tribulation (post-tribulation). I advocate that the Rapture happens at some undetermined point *during* the tribulation period. Since the Great Tribulation does *not* start with the grand-but-invisible entrance of Jesus at the Rapture (pretribulation), the exact start of the Great Tribulation itself will be unknown and is unknowable.

Now that we have names for the two competing doctrines, let's discuss the implications and consequences of each viewpoint.

The Imminent Return of Christ?

Pretribulationists teach (and have been teaching for nearly two hundred years now) that the return of Christ is imminent. They teach that if Christians would begin to understand the shortness of time left, then the church would find newfound enthusiasm for evangelism, and revival would sweep the land. Unfortunately, this has not happened, and the doctrine, for the most part, has had no lasting impact upon people's behavior. For me personally, even when I believed it, this teaching was too abstract to be a daily reality and affect my daily behavior.

However, my daily behavior *is* influenced by my immediate expectations. I expect to be alive tomorrow, so I get up and earn a living each day to prepare for the future. When you are dealing with people in any capacity, setting the proper expectations is one of the most important things you can do.

A multitude of examples could be used to explain this concept. One such example is a restaurant queue. When you arrive at a popular restaurant, you often have to wait for a table. We all ask the same question in this situation: "How long will it be?" I have noticed, on a number of occasions, that restaurants will provide an exaggerated wait time in order to properly set the expectation. When the actual wait time is *less* than anticipated, people are happy. When the actual wait time for a table is much *longer* than anticipated, people become frustrated, angry, and even hostile. Restaurant owners are smart enough to realize that they need to set the expectation so that they rarely exceed the stated wait time.

In this example, the actual table wait time doesn't really matter. What matters is the expectation that people have about when they will be seated. If you set a false expectation, you create a host of problems. Your diners will be hostile before they even order their meals, which often will lead to even more complaints and trouble throughout the visit.

If we apply this concept of expectations to the pretribulation rapture, we can easily see the potential downfall! If we establish the expectation that an individual Christian will not have to endure any of the hardships of the Great Tribulation, we had better be 100 percent correct. Otherwise, Christians may become frustrated, angry, and hostile toward the church, church leaders, and their brothers and sisters in Christ when they realize their expectations have not been met. This is a natural reaction when people feel they have been misled.

Inaccurate expectations also pave the way for deception. If you firmly believe in the pretribulation rapture and never consider other possibilities, then it stands to reason that you may be blind to the events unfolding in the world that suggest something to the contrary. An average church member who never questions the pretribulation rapture doctrine might find it impossible to believe that he is actually living in the Great Tribulation. He may not be able to comprehend that a new charismatic world leader is actually the Antichrist, because he is still looking for Jesus in the Rapture first. The Bible clearly teaches that the Antichrist comes before Christ returns (we'll explore this in later chapters), but if Christians are not expecting this, they might not recognize him. This could allow the Antichrist to easily deceive church members simply because of their firmly rooted belief in a pretribulation rapture. If we are looking only for the return of Christ, we might miss the rise of the Antichrist entirely.

I'm afraid that the pretribulation rapture doctrine is so firmly planted in the minds of many that multitudes will be unable to recognize the lies and deception sweeping the world during the end times. It's hard to admit mistakes, so I'm concerned that many will be unwilling or simply unable to take a step back and review their belief systems in light of the end times. The Bible says in Matthew 24:24 that even the elect will have a hard time deciphering the deception of the Antichrist. I often wonder what will become of our church members who have very little scriptural knowledge. Will they fall prey to the deception?

As you will learn later in this book, the Bible teaches that the church will be heavily persecuted during the Great Tribulation. The freedoms we enjoy in America have buffered us from the concept of such suffering for Christ. However, unless we begin to teach current and future generations that they should expect persecution, they (and we) will not be mentally prepared to deal with the struggle. Second Timothy 3:12 says, "All that will live godly in Christ Jesus shall suffer persecution." It is even conceivable that improperly set expectations regarding the return of Christ could lead to hostile believers, who turn against their own. Jesus foretold such betrayal during the end times.

> Now the brother shall betray the brother to death, and the father the son; and children shall rise up against their parents, and shall cause them to be put to death. (Mark 13:12)

There is also the issue of trustworthiness. If actual end-times events prove that the pretribulation rapture is false, the credibility of much of the church could fairly be called into question. This could lead church members to doubt all aspects of the faith, including the validity and authority of the Bible. The average person might reasonably draw the conclusion that if the church messed up such an important doctrine, then the church is wrong about a host of other things as well. This could result in major spiritual crises for many individuals—at a time when such crises will be especially hard to handle. Church members' expectations will be shattered, and the church will have lost credibility in matters of the faith, both within its walls and without.

As I've outlined earlier in this chapter, the pretribulation rapture doctrine is well-known even outside of the church because of American pop culture. If an unbelieving world thinks that real Christians are to be removed in the Rapture before the Great Tribulation, then it will be nearly impossible to warn unbelievers that they are living in the last days as predicted by Jesus and his prophets and that the new world leader is the Antichrist.

The church will be mocked. I can hear it now: "Why are you even still here? I thought Christ was coming for you!" Second Peter 3:3–4 warns us:

> Knowing this first, that there shall come in the last days scoffers, walking after their own lusts, and saying, Where is the promise of his coming? for since the fathers fell asleep, all things continue as they were from the beginning of the creation.

Far from fanning the flames of evangelism as pretribulation teachers hope to see, this doctrine could cause the slow death of evangelism as the deception of the Antichrist rises. Any of the elect who try to proclaim the truth of the Word of God will be mocked, ridiculed, and ultimately persecuted. The elect may appear to be a bunch of crazy and unstable weirdos because society's expectations about the pretribulation return of Christ were so misplaced.

On the other hand, if we were to replace the pretribulation rapture doctrine with the great tribulation rapture doctrine, there would also be consequences. My hope is that a great tribulation rapture doctrine would begin to prepare the minds of Christians for the end of times and the Great Tribulation, while also having an impact on their current lifestyles.

If we expect to encounter hardship and betrayal during the end times, then our faith will not be easy to shatter. Even though the Bible clearly predicts persecution, American churches have not prepared modern Christians for the persecution and betrayal that will accompany the Great Tribulation. Without the proper mental preparation, the church and the faith of the individual Christian could suffer great harm.

If you study church history, you will quickly learn that many of the previous generations since Christ have believed that they were living in the last generation for one reason or another. Our generation is no different. We all seem to think that "The End is Near" (maybe because of that scruffy guy holding a picket sign on the corner of Main Street). I think it is safe to assume that future generations of Christians also will be of the same mindset. As for me, I believe the end could quickly come because the world has become a much smaller place through travel, business, and technology, which have laid the groundwork needed for many of the prophetic events described in the Bible. But even if I am wrong, not every generation will be. Eventually, one generation of Christians *will* reach the end of time. And they will need to be prepared.

If we do believe we are near the end, then the great tribulation rapture doctrine may be what we need to teach current and future Christians; that the call of obedience to Christ could, within our own lifetimes, demand the ultimate sacrifice of martyrdom. If martyrdom is within your expectations, then serious consideration of your dedication to Christ should follow.

Today, Western society protects us from the fear of religious persecution. I'm afraid this thin veil of protection has caused North American and European Christians to fail to contemplate or consider their individual responses when society and world governments turn against the Christian. Have you thought about how you will respond to the fear and intimidation that accompanies persecution? What happens if you are banned from society, or imprisoned, or even given a death penalty? Will your faith endure through tough times?

An individual's initial commitment to Christ could be likened to a wedding. At a wedding, the vows are exchanged, and the start of the marriage is a cause for great rejoicing. However, the important part of the marriage is in the ongoing commitment to the marriage for a lifetime. While we rejoice in the salvation of the lost, *it is equally important to teach people that a healthy relationship with Christ is an ongoing and daily commitment to him.* In evangelical circles, the emphasis is often on gaining converts by counting the number of people who come forward during an altar call, or who raise their hands in response to the prayer of salvation. But just like a marriage between husband and wife, the commitment to Christ requires effort. Your relationship with God Almighty will only grow stronger if you take the time to develop it. If we would begin to teach people that salvation is not just a get-out-of-hell-free card but a serious commitment to a holy God who needs to be respected and honored even to the point of death, then Christians might begin to put their spiritual lives in proper perspective to the physical world.

My hope is that the great tribulation rapture doctrine as it is laid out in this book will be a catalyst to teaching that obedience to Christ demands sacrifice. This teaching should have immediate consequences, because Christians will need to seriously consider their overall dedication to Jesus Christ and his commandments for the rest of their lives—until death do us part. In addition, the teaching will have future positive consequences, because the individual Christian during the Great Tribulation will be better prepared to follow Christ regardless of the circumstances.

The Call to Repentance

Serious dedication to Christ leads to repentance: turning with contrition from sin to God. *Repentance* is also defined as changing one's mind for the better. In evangelical circles, the emphasis is placed on believing on Jesus Christ. We rarely discuss repentance. In Acts 2, when Peter is giving his first sermon, he states:

> And it shall come to pass, that whosoever shall call on the name of the Lord shall be saved. (Acts 2:21)

As Peter completes his sermon, he is questioned by the audience:

> Now when they heard this, they were pricked in their heart, and said unto Peter and to the rest of the apostles, Men and brethren, what shall we do? Then Peter said unto them, Repent, and be baptized every one of you in the name of Jesus Christ for the remission of sins, and ye shall receive the gift of the Holy Ghost. (Acts 2:37–38)

Notice that when the audience asks what they should do, Peter does not respond with "Whosoever shall call on the name of the Lord shall be saved." Instead, Peter adds to his previous proclamation the requirement to repent, followed by baptism. Calling upon the Lord includes repentance for your sins. Without calling upon the Lord, you will not be led to repentance. Without repentance, the act of calling on the Lord is meaningless. If the church accepts the great tribulation rapture doctrine, realizing that all believers will indeed suffer persecution and will need to be strong in faith and a righteous life, then the call to repentance should become a natural part of our teaching in order to strengthen relationships with God after conversion so that we are prepared for tough times.

Again, the marriage analogy applies. When you get married, you are making a statement that you are no longer eligible to date, that you are making a complete lifestyle change. You have turned from your single life and have started a new, lifelong commitment to your spouse. You have laid aside your old ways and have decided to move forward in your relationship by a strong outward statement of commitment (the wedding) and a willingness to sacrifice for the sake of the union. Repentance is the same way. You must make a break with your old lifestyle and commit to learning and understanding the commandments of God so that you can maintain a healthy spiritual relationship with your Savior. It is exactly that type of committed relationship that is necessary to prepare Christians for the end times.

Preparing for the Antichrist

Another important aspect of the great tribulation rapture doctrine is that the Bible clearly teaches that the Antichrist will be revealed *before* the Rapture (more on this later). This is an important emphasis. A few pastors I know continue to repeat from the pulpit that every prophecy has been fulfilled and the only thing remaining is for Christ to return. It sounds good, but it's not the truth according to Scripture.

If we teach that the church will see the Antichrist revealed, as opposed to being snatched away before he gets here, Christians will be more resistant to the deception of the Antichrist and the many false claims of messiahship in the world. I have heard that the pretribulation rapture is correct because it teaches Christians to look for the return of Christ (i.e. "the blessed hope" of Titus 2:13), and that our focus should be on Christ and not on the arrival of the Antichrist. However, if we take this to its logical conclusion and teach Christians *only* to look for Christ, and then the Rapture does not occur before the Antichrist arrives, believers might not recognize the Antichrist for who he is and could easily fall prey to his deceptions.

On the other hand, if we teach believers that Jesus provided a step-by-step outline that documents the events prior to his return—as he did—we might not be so blind to the start of the Great Tribulation and the nearness of the return of Christ. We will be able to start matching up the prophecies in the Revelation to the daily news reports. We will realize, as world events wax worse and worse, that some of the events line up with the warning signs predicted in Scripture, giving us warning of the end.

If we believe that we will endure hardship, then we will start looking at one another as true believers in Christ, brothers and sisters upon whom we will need to rely in tough times. We might start truly loving one another as commanded by the Bible (John 13:34 and elsewhere) because we'll want to have healthy relationships with our fellow believers so that we can come together in the hard times.

There are many benefits to replacing the pretribulation rapture doctrine with the great tribulation rapture doctrine. My only concern is that future Christians might spend too much time trying to force fit current events into the end-time chronology of the great tribulation rapture doctrine and start prematurely predicting the Great Tribulation or proclaiming that this or that individual is the Antichrist. Like the May 21, 2011, end-of-the-world prediction that came and went without a whimper, false proclamations harden people to the truth and discredit valid Bible teaching. Unfortunately, stereotypes and labels exist and tend to persist in our culture, so we must be vigilant not to embarrass the church with false proclamations of the end.

Of course, benefits to believing something do not make it true. We will get to the scriptural arguments for the great tribulation rapture doctrine in the next chapter. But first, I want to examine one more consequence to wrong belief in the area of the end times.

Psychological Warfare Tactics

When you consider the importance of any rapture doctrine, you must consider its consequences. This is important. I think of it in terms of psychological warfare. Psychological warfare is the use of various techniques to influence a target's morale, beliefs, and behavior. The Bible compares our spiritual struggle to warfare (Eph. 6:12), and psychological warfare is a main weapon of our enemy.

Consider the rapture doctrines from this aspect. Today, there are multitudes of great Christian leaders and pastors with a sincere desire to turn others to Jesus Christ and help them find true life in God, but their lifetime efforts could be damaged if the pretribulation rapture does not occur as they have taught and the Great Tribulation starts instead. The pretribulation rapture doctrine, because it influences people's beliefs, emotions, and reasoning, could have a devastating effect if it is wrong (and it is). The individual Christian, being unprepared, could fall right in line with what our enemy desires. In the end, the pretribulation rapture doctrine could cause great damage to the cause of Christ and negatively impact many believers.

So you should ask yourself this: if you were Satan, what would you want the church to believe about the timing of the Rapture? Which doctrine would you want the vast majority of Christians and non-Christians to believe? Which doctrine could you gain the most benefit from?

The answer is clearly the pretribulation rapture doctrine. If the church and the unbelieving world expect a pretribulation rapture and it does not occur, Satan will have effectively discredited the church from within and paved the way for Antichrist in the world. Once the Great Tribulation begins, the natural consequences of misguided expectations will take effect.

Study to Show Thyself Approved

Have we accepted what we have been taught simply because we have put our faith and trust in the teachers of God's Word rather than exploring the Scriptures for ourselves? Have we come to believe that our teachers, pastors, and scholars are 100 percent right in all matters of doctrine? Do we believe that no false doctrine exists in our churches today? Have we come to rely more on the opinions of the "experts" than on our own study of God's Word?

> Study to shew thyself approved unto God, a workman that needeth not to be ashamed, rightly dividing the word of truth. (2 Tim. 2:15)

My hope is that as you continue this study of the Scriptures with me, you will take the time to consider the implications of rapture doctrine for the last generation. Make your decision based on the Scriptures and your own communion with God. We owe it to our future brothers and sisters in Christ. The consequences for misguided expectations are enormous.

I'll end this chapter with these Scriptures:

"Now the Spirit speaketh expressly, that in the *latter times* some shall depart from the faith, giving heed to seducing spirits, and doctrines of devils; take heed unto thyself, and unto the doctrine; continue in them: for in doing this thou shalt both save thyself, and them that hear thee." (1 Tim. 4:1, 16, emphasis mine)

But there were false prophets also among the people, even as there shall be false teachers among you, who privily shall bring in damnable heresies, even denying the Lord that bought them, and bring upon themselves swift destruction. (2 Pet. 2:1)

Prove all things; hold fast that which is good. (1 Thess. 5:21)

"It ain't what you don't know that gets you into trouble. It's what you know for sure that just ain't so."—Mark Twain

Chapter 2

WHAT ARE THE SIGNS OF HIS COMING? A CHRONOLOGICAL STEP-BY-STEP ANSWER

So now we begin the study of the great tribulation rapture doctrine as it is laid out in Scripture. From here, I've outlined the chronological nature of the end-time events leading up to the rapture of the saints. The chronology begins with a conversation between Jesus and his disciples.

Like many of us today, the disciples were interested in the end times. On one occasion, they questioned the Son of God about the future. Consider these Scriptures and the context of their question:

THE QUESTION

Matthew 24:3	Luke 21:7	Mark 13:4
And as he sat upon the mount of Olives, the disciples came unto him privately, saying, Tell us, when shall these things be? *and* what shall be the sign of thy coming, *and of* the end of the world?	*And they asked him saying, Master, but when shall these things be? and* sign *will there be when these things shall come to pass?*	Tell us, when *shall these things be? and* what shall be the sign *when all these things shall be fulfilled*

Matthew recorded the question specifically. The disciples plainly asked Christ to provide the signs of his coming and the signs of the end of the world.

Did Jesus answer these disciples, "Sorry, I can't tell you anything"? If he did, then there is nothing to report, and a secret surprise rapture would be a valid doctrine to consider—in other words, his coming would have no signs. However, Jesus did not avoid the question, which puts a damper on the pretribulation rapture doctrine and its heavy reliance upon the secret, imminent return of Christ at any moment, without any chronological signs preceding or pointing to it. Rather, Jesus answered the question in great detail.

Years later, Jesus returned to John in a vision and provided even more details regarding the signs of his coming and the end of the world. We call this book the Revelation, and it is self-defined as "the Revelation of Jesus Christ."

> The Revelation of Jesus Christ, which God gave unto him, to shew unto his servants things which must shortly come to pass; and he sent and signified it by his angel unto his servant John. (Rev. 1:1)

Notice that the purpose of the Revelation is to show the servants of Christ the things which must come to pass. We are meant to know the signs of his coming and of the end of the world. God is not the author of confusion (1 Cor. 14:33). God is trying to clearly communicate to his church what we need to watch for and what we should expect at the end.

In answer to the disciples' direct question, Jesus' answer provides a detailed and chronological order for the signs that we need to consider. The chronological nature of these events is a key to this study—and it is self-evident in the Bible. Throughout the parallel accounts in Matthew, Mark, and Luke, there are numerous occasions where the events are plainly stated to be in chronological order. Look at the wording in these passages (emphasis mine):

Matthew 24:8: "BEGINNING of sorrows"
Matthew 24:9: "THEN shall"
Matthew 24:14: "AND THEN shall the end come"
Matthew 24:15: "WHEN ye therefore shall see"
Matthew 24:21: "FOR THEN shall be"
Matthew 24:29: "IMMEDIATELY AFTER"

Matthew 24:30: "AND THEN"
Luke 21:8b: "And the TIME DRAWETH NEAR"
Luke 21:12: "But BEFORE ALL THESE"
Luke 21:20: "And WHEN ye shall see"
Luke 21:25: "AND there shall be"
Luke 21:27: "AND THEN"
Mark 31:8b: "the BEGINNINGS of sorrows"
Mark 13:10: "MUST FIRST"
Mark 13:14: "But WHEN ye shall see"
Mark 13:19: "For in THOSE DAYS"
Mark 13:24: "But in those days, AFTER THAT"
Mark 13:26: "AND THEN"
Mark 13:27: "AND THEN"

We cannot escape the fact that Jesus' answer to the disciples is a step-by-step warning of the things to come before his return. There can be no doubt that this is a chronological listing of events. God, the author, has listed the events in plain and simple order as they will unfold. This is not meant to be confusing. These are the signs that we should watch for.

Chapter 3

The First Warning: Take Heed, Pay Attention, Do Not Be Deceived

Jesus begins with a strong warning. He commands his disciples to watch for deception regarding the teaching about his return. This call to attention is for each of us. We are commanded to be vigilant so that no false doctrine surrounding the signs of his return or the end of the world find their way into our beliefs. Jesus starts his answer with this command and ends his answer with this command.

The Beginning

Matthew 24:4	Luke 21:8a	Mark 13:5
And Jesus answered and said unto them, Take heed *that* no man *deceive you.*	*And he said,* Take heed *that ye be not* be not deceived	*And Jesus answering them began to say,* Take heed lest any *man* deceive you.

This is a key starting point for the Lord. I find it interesting that Jesus begins by warning that we "be not deceived" by any man. We often overlook the fact that the experts we rely upon are mere men. As human beings, we often value the "expert" opinion more than we should. The warning against deception applies equally to laypersons, the world at large, and our well-meaning clergy and teachers.

In most evangelical and Bible-believing churches, the pretribulation rapture doctrine is rarely if ever debated. Christians belonging to these segments of the church body often have accepted the doctrine without proof and without discussion because many leaders do not allow for open debate—whether by deliberately squelching it or simply by failing to provide a forum for it.

However, false doctrine often finds its way into our preaching. Take the following Scripture from Matthew 24 as an example:

> "Now learn a parable of the fig tree; when his branch is yet tender, and putteth forth leaves, ye know that summer is nigh: so likewise ye, when ye shall see all these things, know that IT IS NEAR, EVEN AT THE DOORS. Verily I say unto you, This generation shall not pass, till all these things be fulfilled. Heaven and earth shall pass away, but my words shall not pass away. (Matt. 24:32–35)

When I was a teenager during the 1980s, it was very popular to teach that the fig tree mentioned in Matthew 24:32 represented the rebirth of the nation of Israel. (Israel became a nation again in 1948.) The church taught that a biblical generation was typically forty years long. Based on the false assumption that the fig tree meant the rebirth of the nation of Israel, the church was fond of teaching that the generation alive during 1948 would see the return of Christ in the Rapture. As we approached the forty-year mark in 1988, this idea became more prominent in many sermons. Many proclaimed the imminent return of Christ. There was even a popular book published called *88 Reasons Jesus Returns in 1988*.

Needless to say, 1988 came and went, as well as the decades since. The generation that saw Israel become a nation in 1948 is getting quite long in the tooth. Since time has proven that this doctrine was false, the preaching on this subject has been abandoned and is now rarely if ever mentioned.

This example points directly to that first command of Jesus: take heed that no man deceive you. It is unfortunate that preachers and teachers I grew up learning under in the 1980s were guilty of deceiving the church in this matter. It was a popular thing to preach because it was pleasing to hear, and there was so much support for it—many of the experts of the day were saying the same thing. At the time, it seemed no one questioned the validity of the statements linking the fig tree parable to the rebirth of the nation of Israel.

I cannot fault preachers for falling into this trap, since the doctrine was so prevalent. However, they failed to take heed of possible deception regarding the return of Christ. As a result, the credibility of the church suffered. Jesus knew there would be false doctrines regarding his return, which is why he started his own discourse on the last days with this warning.

Parrots, Not Preachers

I fear that many well-meaning preachers fall into the trap of believing everything they hear from the pulpit, from other ministers, from seminary teachers, and from "experts" of various kinds. As lay Christians, we often look to the man in the pulpit and assume that he has all the facts well documented, checked out, and backed firmly by Scripture. I suspect that our leaders often assume the same thing about each other! When our pastors and teachers hear something in a sermon that catches their attention, the habit is to take the same information and teach it to their congregations without questioning its validity. Many pastors just parrot what they hear or read from other pastors. If it sounds good and comes from a "credible source," then they are likely to accept the information as fact and pass it along to their congregations.

The 1980s rapture doctrine should serve as an example to all who preach, teach, and listen to God's Word that we need to be searching the Scriptures on our own in order to ensure that what we communicate regarding his Word can be backed up by his Word.

While adherents of both pretribulation and post-tribulation doctrine use Scripture to support their cases, they fail to provide an explanation for their teaching using the entire context of Scripture; therefore, each fails to discredit the alternate view. Any limited debate goes back and forth without resolution. This creates confusion, and Satan loves confusion.

While you review the great tribulation rapture evidence presented here, you'll begin to see how easily all of the end-time Scriptures fit together when you abandon the pretribulation rapture idea. Once the timing of the Rapture is understood correctly, many difficult passages in the Bible become clear, and the end-time chronology becomes easy to see.

But I hope you won't just take my word for it. As you read on, I pray that you will read with your Bible open and your mind firmly grounded in the whole counsel of Scripture.

Chapter 4

THE FIRST THREE SIGNS: DECEPTION, WAR, AND THE BEGINNING OF SORROWS

The first sign Jesus provides is an increase in deception. As the time draws near, there will be many who will come in the names of Jesus, Messiah, and Christ. These con artists will deceive many. Jesus warns us not to follow after them.

THE FIRST SIGN: DECEPTION

Matthew 24:5	Luke 21:8b	Mark 13:6
For many shall come in my name, saying, I am Christ; and shall deceive many.	*For Many shall come in my name, saying I am Christ; and the draweth near: go ye not therefore after them.*	*For many shall come in my name, saying, I am Christ; and shall deceive many.*

The number of people claiming to be Christ is on the rise. From the first to the eighteenth century, approximately twenty-seven people were self-proclaimed Christs. This number rose to approximately thirty-six people making the claim during the nineteenth and twentieth centuries. In the last two hundred years alone, the number of people claiming to be Christ has exceeded the total number of people claiming to be Christ during the previous eighteen hundred years![7]

In the nineteenth century, nine people claimed to be Christ. In the twentieth century, twenty-seven people made the claim, which is a 300 percent increase! The first sign of deception is already playing out and will continue to accelerate to the end.

Many of these self-proclaimed Christs deceive others into following them, even to the death. For example, a man named Dr. Jose Luis De Jesus Miranda, sixty-one, spoke to an amphitheater filled with his followers in Orlando, Florida, in 2007. This gathering represented only a handful of his millions of followers. This man claims he is Jesus Christ incarnate. His followers believe that Miranda's life and teachings replace those of Jesus, and they often tattoo their bodies with "666" in belief that the second coming of Christ has taken place.[8]

The Bible is very clear that there is only one Jesus Christ. His return will be marked with great fanfare, including the sound of a trumpet, angels, and lightning. Yet, many people will continue to be deceived by false Christs.

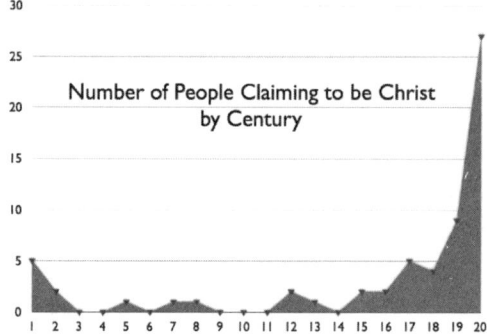

I am always amazed at the number of followers a self-proclaimed Christ can gather. Jesus Christ proclaimed himself as the Son of God and equal to God, but he had the miracles to back it up! Jesus raised people from the dead, healed the lame, gave sight to the blind, restored hearing to the deaf, cleansed the lepers, walked on water, calmed the storm, and predicted that he would rise from the dead—and then did it.

> Now when John had heard in the prison the works of Christ, he sent two of his disciples, and said unto him, Art thou he that should come, or do we look for another? Jesus answered and said unto them, Go and shew John again those things which ye do hear and see: The blind receive their sight, and the lame walk, the lepers are cleansed, and the deaf hear, the dead are raised up, and the poor

have the gospel preached to them. And blessed is he, whosoever shall not be offended in me. (Matt. 11:2–6)

Jesus also had the entire bulk of Old Testament prophecy concerning the Messiah behind him—prophecy that he completely and perfectly fulfilled during his birth, life, death, and resurrection. The fulfillment of many of these prophecies could not be manufactured, such as being born in Bethlehem or growing up in Galilee—not to mention rising from the dead!

The false Christs, by contrast, are not able to prove their claims. All they have are words and charisma. Often with questionable backgrounds, these false Christs are able to convince many that they are the return of Jesus Christ. Dr. Jose Luis De Jesus Miranda was able to attract enough followers to fill an amphitheater. Each of these followers is an individual soul whom God Almighty loves and cherishes. God has warned all of us not to follow after people claiming to be Christ. Yet people ignore the warnings posted in the Word of God and blindly follow after a charismatic leader.

Jesus warns us that as the end of time draws near, there will be more and more men claiming to be the Christ, or Messiah. Notice that in Luke 21:8b, the first sign is just the beginning. The growing number of people claiming to be Christ is proof that the time is drawing near. The Rapture cannot occur until the other signs are fulfilled as well, but we should take note that the first sign Jesus provided is already being fulfilled during our lifetimes. A 300 percent increase in false Christ proclamations over the last one hundred years is certainly noteworthy.

The Second Sign: Multiple Wars

The second sign is well-known to most Christians because it is often the most-referenced sign. This is the sign of wars and rumors of wars. War is easy to remember because of the fanfare, the media publicity, and the destruction that wars ultimately create. Jesus continued the chronological narrative as follows:

The Second Sign: War

Matthew 24:6	Luke 21:9	Mark 13:7
And ye shall hear of wars and rumours of wars: see that ye be not troubled: for all these things must come to pass, but the end is not yet.	*But when ye shall hear of wars and commotions, be not terrified: for these things must first come to pass; but the end is not by and by.*	*And when ye shall hear of wars and rumours of wars, be ye not troubled: for such things must needs be; but the end shall not be yet.*

Jesus told us that the world near the end of time would be full of war. At the time of this writing (2011), there are forty-two active wars or political conflicts in the world.[9]

Many other rumors of war are reported weekly, including many of the conflicts currently labeled as "the Arab Spring."

Mark Harrison and Nikolaus Wolf, professors from the University of Warwick and Humboldt University, conducted a study on the increasing frequency of wars. Their research indicates that war between states increased 6 percent per year between 1870–1913, 17 percent per year during the time period that included the two World Wars, and 31 percent per year during the Cold War era. In the 1990s, the frequency of wars between states rose by 36 percent per year.[10]

The war trend is on the rise.

Even as the second sign is being fulfilled, we must remember Jesus clearly stated that the "end is not yet." Jesus said the increase in wars "must first come to pass." Again, this points to the chronological nature of the answer Jesus provided when asked, "What is the sign of thy coming and the end of the world?" While the claims of false Christs and the increase in wars continue, other things must happen before the return of Jesus and the end of the world. Jesus provides these additional signs as he continues to explain to the disciples what will come to pass.

The Third Sign: The Beginning of Sorrows

Matthew 24:7–8	Luke 21:10–11a	Mark 13:8
For nation shall rise against nation, and kingdom against kingdom: and there shall be famines, and pestilences, and earthquakes, in divers places. All these are the beginning of sorrows.	*Then said he unto them, Nation shall rise against nation, and kingdom: and great earthquakes shall be in divers places, and famines, and pestilences.*	*For nation shall rise against nation, and kingdom against kingdom: and there shall be earthquakes in divers places, and there shall be famines and troubles: these are the beginnings of of sorrows.*

The beginning of sorrows is the third sign. Merriam-Webster defines "sorrow" as "a deep distress, sadness, or regret especially for the loss of someone or something loved." Jesus describes war, famine, pestilences, and earthquakes as the beginning of sorrows. It is obvious that there will be substantial loss of life based on these events. Jesus also defines this as the beginning, or the start, of an event or process.

In reality, this is the beginning of the Great Tribulation. The first two signs we reviewed (false Christs and the rise in war) are indications that the Great Tribulation is approaching. The third sign is the start of the Great Tribulation itself.

The exact start of "the beginning of sorrows" will be difficult to determine. The start of the Great Tribulation is not marked by the return of Christ at the Rapture and a cataclysmic disappearance of millions, as the pretribulation rapture doctrine predicts. Rather, the beginning of sorrows will come upon the world rather subtly. (This is why it is impossible to predict the exact date of the Rapture, as midtrib doctrine attempts to do.) It will be documented in the daily newspaper but will appear to be the typical news of death and destruction to which we have grown accustomed.

Gospel Signs and the Revelation

If you take a closer look at the Scripture, you will see that the signs Jesus provides in the three gospel accounts correspond to the end-times account in the Revelation. In the Gospels, Jesus provided the highlights, the executive summary, of the end times to his disciples. Later on, Jesus revisited John and gave a more detailed description of what the church should expect.

From this point forward, I will begin to compare the Gospels and the Revelation to demonstrate how closely the events match. *You will also begin to see that they follow one another in chronological fashion as a sequence of events.* This is one of the keys that discredits the idea of a pretribulation rapture prior to the Great Tribulation. In the Gospels, Jesus clearly states that these events must *first* come to pass before his return in the Rapture.

In the Gospels, after Jesus is done explaining the signs and giving a complete description of the Rapture to the disciples, the discussion ends. There is nothing left for Jesus to explain to the church because we are gone; we are raptured away. Jesus directly answered the question the disciples asked: "What is the sign of thy coming and of the end of the world?" Revelation finishes the story of what occurs on the earth after the church has been removed. These future events include the vial judgments, full of the wrath of God, and Armageddon.

In the Gospels, Jesus highlights four events described as the beginning of sorrows. In Revelation, the first four seal judgments also include four events. The comparison is too close to ignore.

The Four Events in the Gospels	The Four Seal Judgments in Revelation
War	World Leader
Famine	War
Pestilence	Famine
Earthquakes	Pestilence

The next section groups the Scriptures per event, so you can compare the beginning of sorrows in the gospel accounts to the four seals in Revelation.

Seal #1: World Leader

Revelation 6:1–2: "And I saw when the Lamb opened one of the seals, and I heard, as it were the noise of thunder, one of the four beasts saying, Come and see. And I saw, and behold a white horse: and he that sat on him had a bow; and a crown was given unto him: and he went forth conquering, and to conquer."

Seal #2: War

Matthew 24:7: "For nation shall rise against nation, and kingdom against kingdom."

Luke 21:10: "Then said he unto them, Nation shall rise against nation, and kingdom against kingdom."

Mark 13:8: "For nation shall rise against nation, and kingdom against kingdom."

Revelation 6:3–4: "And when he had opened the second seal, I heard the second beast say, Come and see. And there went out another horse that was red: and power was given to him that sat thereon to take peace from the earth, and that they should kill one another: and there was given unto him a great sword."

Seal #3: Famine

Matthew 24:7: "And there shall be famines."

Luke 21:11: "And famines."

Mark 13:8: "And there shall be famines and troubles."

Revelation 6:5–6: "And when he had opened the third seal, I heard the third beast say, Come and see. And I beheld, and lo a black horse; and he that sat on him had a pair of balances in his hand. And I heard a voice in the midst of the four beasts say, A measure of wheat for a penny, and three measures of barley for a penny; and see thou hurt not the oil and the wine."

Seal #4: Pestilence

Matthew 24:7: "And pestilences."

Luke 21:11: "And pestilences."

Revelation 6:7–8: "And when he had opened the fourth seal, I heard the voice of the fourth beast say, Come and see. And I looked, and behold a pale horse: and his name that sat on him was Death, and Hell followed with him. And power was given unto them over the fourth part of the earth, to kill with sword, and with hunger, and with death, and with the beasts of the earth."

Earthquakes

Matthew 24:7: "And earthquakes, in divers places."
Luke 21:11: "And great earthquakes shall be in divers places."
Mark 13:8: "And there shall be earthquakes in divers places."

The Beginning of Sorrows

Matthew 24:8: "All these are the beginning of sorrows."
Mark 13:8: "These are the beginnings of sorrows."

All of these events are described by the Gospels as the beginning of sorrows. This is the start of the Great Tribulation. During this time period, there will be great loss of life. The fourth seal describes Death riding a pale horse, with Hell following close behind. Death has power over one-fourth of the earth. I've heard it taught that one-fourth of the world's population will die here, but I'm inclined to believe that the pale horse is given authority over one-fourth of the *earth* (and not over one-fourth of the earth's *population*). Therefore, the pale horse does not directly affect the other three-quarters of the earth. For example, let's pretend that Africa is exactly one-fourth of the earth (it's not, but the gross caricature works for purposes of illustration). If the pale horse rides in Africa, then the rest of the world will get to watch the horror on TV. Regardless, no matter how you interpret this, there will be substantial loss of life, signifying the start of a deep distress.

The Seal Judgments

The first seal in the Revelation states that power will be given to a leader who is able to go forth and conquer. Whenever a leader is elevated and has plans to go forth and conquer, history shows that his power is resisted. This world leader also will be resisted and will produce the natural effect of most political conflicts: war. The second seal takes peace from the earth, and war is rampant. War is devastating to society because it destroys the means of production and distribution, including the production and distribution of food and other necessary products. The natural effect of war is the third seal, famine. The fourth seal is death. The Bible says these combined events lead to a great loss of life.

As the seals progressively get more severe, many will turn to God. We have seen something like this happen before: in America, after 9/11, the churches were full. People came to church for prayer and consolation. When massive numbers of deaths occur at the start of the Great Tribulation, many will turn to the church. The church will grow, and the gospel will spread rapidly and with ease. And it just so happens that the next sign Jesus provides in the Gospels corresponds to the natural effect of a growing and awakened church: an evangelism explosion.

Lulled to Sleep

When it comes to end-times doctrine, the problem for the church in Western society is that we may not recognize the start of the Great Tribulation when it arrives. Since many have been taught a false doctrine concerning the timing of the Rapture, they may not recognize these events as the beginning of sorrows and the start of the Great Tribulation.

I believe that Western society is being lulled to sleep by current events and history. If you look back over the course of history, you can see that the world is full of war, famine, pestilence, and earthquakes. Consider all the horrors you learned about in history class, such as the Black Plague, the Potato Famine, World Wars I and II, the multiple famines in Africa, and many more. I could compile a list of events like these that could go on for pages.

Meanwhile, we are bombarded daily with news reports that describe other horrors. For example, we quickly learn (and just as quickly forget) about an earthquake in Haiti that kills one hundred fifty thousand people in a matter of moments. Our daily lives are not affected by the pestilence that subsequently ravages the survivors in Haiti. We simply move on.

We read news reports of a volcanic eruption in Iceland that blocks out the sun for days and weeks and disrupts air travel in Europe, but Americans barely notice because it does not affect our daily lives. Even as I write this book, the pace of disasters seems to be growing. Japan has suffered a 9.0 earthquake, followed by a tsunami and then a nuclear meltdown. Fertile Japanese farmland is now polluted with salt from the ocean that will diminish crop yield for years to come. In the spring of 2011, the central United States suffered the largest tornado outbreak in history with hundreds of deaths. It was unprecedented. The Middle Eastern nations are in a state of unrest, and civilians are being killed by their governments during protests. The United States is in two protracted wars (three if you count dropping bombs on Libya).

It appears to me that the pace and intensity of disasters are increasing, and my natural reaction is to become desensitized. And this proves the importance of correct doctrine regarding the end times. If we become immune to the horrors around us and we falsely believe that Jesus will return before things get *really* bad, there is a good chance we will not recognize the start of the first four seals as they are described in Revelation. While the beginning of sorrows will be more intense than what we see from day to day, I'm concerned that it will appear to be no different from all the previous events we have read about in our newspapers over the decades.

We are like a lobster that is slowly being boiled in a pot. The water starts out cold and slowly warms to a boil, and the lobster does not react. The same will happen with the world events around us that slowly heat to a boil as described in the Gospels and the first four seal judgments. However, many Christians are so secure and confident in the assertion that the Rapture will happen prior to the Great Tribulation that the church and her leaders (at least in North America) will be unaware of what is unfolding, and they could fail to react. Many will find it difficult to consider that we have truly entered the end of times.

Comfort in the Great Tribulation

As I've studied the Bible in regard to the end times, a few verses have taken on a whole new meaning for me. The Great Tribulation will bring war, famine, and pestilence (disease). If you believe this could happen during your lifetime, you might decide to stockpile food, build a fort, dig a hole, get off the grid, shop more frequently at Cabela's, move to North Dakota, and hunker down. However, I think the Bible offers a better way: trust in God to provide. Look at what the Psalms record for those who fear God and hope in his mercy:

> Behold, the eye of the LORD is upon them that fear him, upon them that hope in his mercy; to deliver their soul from death, and *to keep them alive in famine.* (Ps. 33:18–19, emphasis mine)

If I ever experience a famine during my lifetime, then my plan is to trust God! Nothing more and nothing less. I believe him. I'll continue to fear him and hope in his mercy. In exchange, I have complete confidence that God will deliver me from death and keep me alive during famine.

Another passage that has taken on a whole new meaning for me is Psalm 91. If you can, take a minute to mentally imagine yourself in a time and place where the first four seal judgments are taking place, particularly the war, famine, and pestilence. Then read Psalm 91 and see how this Scripture provides comfort:

> He that dwelleth in the secret place of the most High shall abide under the shadow of the Almighty. I will say of the LORD, He is my refuge and my fortress: *my God; in him will I trust.* Surely he shall deliver thee from the snare of the fowler, and from the noisome pestilence. (Ps. 91:1–3, emphasis mine)

Here, God is stating his plan for those who trust him. If you trust him, he will deliver you, even from the pestilence. Psalm 91 continues:

> He shall cover thee with his feathers, and under his wings shalt thou trust: his truth shall be thy shield and buckler. (Ps. 91:4)

Again, we have a promise of protection if we trust him. Part of trusting God is believing in the truth written in the Word of God.

> Thou shalt not be afraid for the terror by night; nor for the arrow that flieth by day; nor for the pestilence that walketh in darkness; nor for the destruction that wasteth at noonday. A thousand shall fall at thy side, and ten thousand at thy right hand; but it shall not come nigh thee. Only with thine eyes shalt thou behold and see the reward of the wicked. (Ps. 91:5–8)

The Bible promises that if I trust in God, I will not be afraid of the terror at night, or the war, or the disease, or the destruction all around me. The Bible says that even if a thousand fall at my side, and ten thousand at my right hand (meaning that death and destruction are very close to me), it will not touch me. But I will see firsthand the reward for wickedness. Psalm 91 continues with more words of comfort:

> Because thou hast made the LORD, which is my refuge, even the most High, thy habitation; there shall no evil befall thee, neither shall any plague come nigh thy dwelling. For he shall give his angels charge over thee, to keep thee in all thy ways. (Ps. 91:9–11)

Again, the qualifier is that I must make the LORD my refuge and habitation. If I live up to this requirement, then no evil will overtake me, and no plague will come into my house, because God's angels will be watching over me and will keep all my ways. Once you insert Psalm 91 into the events described at the beginning of the Great Tribulation, the passage takes on a whole new meaning and becomes real and applicable. The call of God does not change. We need to trust him, believe him, and rely upon him.

Chapter 5

THE FOURTH SIGN: WORLDWIDE GOSPEL WITNESS

With the fourth sign, the Gospels and the Revelation follow along in sequence with each other yet again. The fourth sign mentioned by Jesus points to worldwide evangelism, when the gospel will be preached and published among all nations. In parallel, Revelation 7 describes 144,000 Jews being sealed as the servants of our God. We will see how this relates in a moment.

THE FOURTH SIGN: THE WORLDWIDE GOSPEL WITNESS

Matthew 24:14	Mark 13:10
And this gospel of the kingdom shall be preached in all the world for a witness unto all nations; and then *shall the end come.*	*And the gospel* must first be *published among all nations.*

And after these things I saw four angels standing on the four corners of the earth, holding the four winds of the earth, that the wind should not blow on the earth, nor on the sea, nor on any tree. And I saw another angel ascending from the east, having the seal of the living God: and he cried with a loud voice to the four angels, to whom it was given to hurt the earth and the sea, saying, Hurt not the earth, neither the sea, nor the trees, till we have sealed the servants of our God in their foreheads. And I heard the number of them which were sealed: and there were sealed an hundred and forty and four thousand of all the tribes of the children of Israel. (Rev. 7:1–4)

While the beginning of sorrows draws people to church, God also has a plan for the Jews that includes the famous 144,000. In Revelation 7, God seals 144,000, twelve thousand from each of the twelve tribes of Israel. These 144,000 are further described in Revelation 14 as the firstfruits unto God and the Lamb. They are virgin men who have been set apart by God for his purpose.

> And I looked, and, lo, a Lamb stood on the mount Sion, and with him an hundred forty and four thousand, having his Father's name written in their foreheads. And I heard a voice from heaven, as the voice of many waters, and as the voice of a great thunder: and I heard the voice of harpers harping with their harps: and they sung as it were a new song before the throne, and before the four beasts, and the elders: and no man could learn that song but the hundred and forty and four thousand, which were redeemed from the earth. These are they which were not defiled with women; for they are virgins. These are they which follow the Lamb whithersoever he goeth. These were redeemed from among men, being the firstfruits unto God and to the Lamb. And in their mouth was found no guile: for they are without fault before the throne of God. (Rev. 14:1–5)

Revelation 14 goes on to describe an angel proclaiming the everlasting gospel (v. 6). This angel warns the inhabitants of the earth of the choice that must be made. Each individual must either keep the commandments of God and the faith of Jesus (v. 12) or worship the beast and receive the mark of the beast in his forehead or hand (vv. 9–10).

> And I saw another angel fly in the midst of heaven, having the everlasting gospel to preach unto them that dwell on the earth, and to every nation, and kindred, and tongue, and people, saying with a loud voice, Fear God, and give glory to him; for the hour of his judgment is come: and worship him that made heaven, and earth, and the sea, and the fountains of waters. And there followed another angel, saying, Babylon is fallen, is fallen, that great city, because she made all nations drink of the wine of the wrath of her fornication.

And the third angel followed them, saying with a loud voice, If any man worship the beast and his image, and receive his mark in his forehead, or in his hand, The same shall drink of the wine of the wrath of God, which is poured out without mixture into the cup of his indignation; and he shall be tormented with fire and brimstone in the presence of the holy angels, and in the presence of the Lamb: and the smoke of their torment ascendeth up for ever and ever: and they have no rest day nor night, who worship the beast and his image, and whosoever receiveth the mark of his name.

Here is the patience of the saints: here are they that keep the commandments of God, and the faith of Jesus. And I heard a voice from heaven saying unto me, Write, Blessed are the dead which die in the Lord from henceforth: Yea, saith the Spirit, that they may rest from their labours; and their works do follow them. (Rev. 14:6–13)

The spiritual battle lines are drawn here at the fourth sign. The Antichrist (the Beast) has come to the world scene as the world leader presented with the very first seal as the conqueror on the white horse. The unbelievers, led by Antichrist, will be offended by the preaching and teaching of Jesus Christ and the cross. The Bible teaches in 1 Corinthians 1:18 that "the preaching of the cross is to them that perish foolishness." As the Antichrist gains power, God grants him the power to destroy the saints for a period of time.

At this point, each individual is given a difficult choice. We must choose to either follow God and have faith in the truth of the Bible or to follow Antichrist. The problem is that following God will be difficult. For some, the choice to follow God and continue in the faith of Jesus Christ will result in premature death. They will become martyrs. Here is the patience of the saints. Here are they that keep the commandments of God. Here is the faith of Jesus.

The preaching of the everlasting gospel to the world will lead to resistance from the world and her governments. The resistance of governments to evangelism, and the growing power of the Antichrist, leads to the natural result: persecution. And as it happens, severe persecution is the fifth sign Jesus provides in the Gospels.

Chapter 6

THE FIFTH SIGN: PERSECUTION

The Gospels provide a detailed description of the persecution of the saints during the Great Tribulation. If you believe the words of Jesus to be true, then you should begin to prepare your heart and mind for what our future on this earth will hold—including the persecution on the horizon.

This know also, that in the last days perilous times shall come… Yea, and all that will live godly in Christ Jesus shall suffer persecution. But evil men and seducers shall wax worse and worse, deceiving, and being deceived. (2 Tim. 3:1, 12–13)

In the last days, *all* who live godly will suffer persecution. That is a blanket statement made by the Word of God over two thousand years ago. If you put this prediction into the context of a prevailing negative attitude toward the gospel of Jesus Christ because of worldwide preaching (the fourth sign), you will realize that persecution is the logical fifth sign described by Jesus.

THE FIFTH SIGN: PERSECUTION

Matthew 24:9–13	Luke 21:12–19	Mark 13:9, 11–13
Then *shall they deliver you up to be afflicted, and shall kill you: and ye shall be hated of all nations for my name's sake. And then shall many be offended, and shall betray one another,*	*But* before all these [Luke 11b: "and fearful sights and great signs shall there be from heaven"—same as the sixth seal in the Revelation], *they shall lay their hands on you,*	*But take heed to yourselves: for they shall deliver you up to councils; and in the synagogues ye shall be beaten: and ye shall be brought before rulers and kings for my sake,*

Matthew 24:9–13	Luke 21:12–19	Mark 13:9, 11–13
and shall hate one another. And many false prophets shall rise, and shall deceive many. And because iniquity shall abound, the love of many shall wax cold. But he that shall endure unto the end, the same shall be saved.	and persecute you, delivering you up to they synagogues, and into prisons, being brought before kings and rulers for my name's sake. And it shall turn to you for a testimony. Settle it therefore in your hearts, not to meditate before what ye shall answer: For I will give you a mouth and wisdom, which all your adversaries shall not be able to gainsay nor resist. And ye shall be betrayed both by parents, and brethren, and kinsfolks, and friends and some of you shall they cause to be put to death. And ye shall be hated of all men for my name's sake. But there shall not an hair of your head perish. In your patience possess ye your souls.	for a testimony against them. But when they shall lead you, and deliver you up, take no thought beforehand what ye shall speak, neither do you premeditate: but whatsoever shall be given you in that hour, that speak ye: for it is not ye that speak, but the Holy Ghost. Now the brother to death, and the father the son; and children shall rise up against their parents, and shall cause them to be put to death. And ye shall be hated of all men for my name's sake: but he that shall endure unto the end, the same shall be saved.

Before I move on, I would like to call your attention to Mark 13:11: "For it is not ye that speak, but the Holy Ghost." The pretribulation rapture doctrine typically teaches that 2 Thessalonians 2:7 is the removal of the Holy Ghost from the earth (2 Thess. 2:7: "For the mystery of iniquity doth already work: only he who now letteth will let, until he be taken out of the way"). The logic is that if the Holy Ghost is removed from the earth, then the church will be taken to heaven, which means the Rapture will take place before the Great Tribulation.

Now, here is where it gets interesting: if you support the pretribulation rapture as it is commonly taught, then you will try to argue that the signs Jesus provides in the Gospels happen *after* the Rapture and that the return of Jesus as described in the Gospels is actually the second coming of Christ and not the Rapture at all. However, you likely also believe that the Holy Ghost is removed at the Rapture. But Mark 13:11 says that the Holy Ghost is *present* during the persecution and will give believers the words to speak. So is the Holy Ghost removed from the earth, or is he still here?

If the Holy Ghost truly is removed at the Rapture, then Mark 13:11 must happen before the Rapture, which means the gospel accounts are leading up to the Rapture. If you say that the Holy Ghost is still here even after the Rapture, then you are taking one of the main arguments to support the pretribulation rapture doctrine away, as 2 Thessalonians 2:7 can no longer apply. The pretribulation rapture doctrine contains other logical flaws as well, which I will point out in the course of this book.

Pattern of Persecution

Notice the pattern of what we should expect: We will be hated of all nations. We will be afflicted and persecuted. Some will be put to death. We will be betrayed by friends and family, parents, children, extended family, etc. We will be hated by all men. We will be jailed. We will be brought before kings and rulers, where the Holy Ghost will speak through us.

But the most important thing to notice in these Scriptures is the call of Jesus. Jesus tells us that if we endure until the end, we will be saved (Matt. 24:13; Mark 13:13). I'm not going to spend time discussing the doctrine of "once saved, always saved," but I am going to ask you to think about the implications of these verses. My own inclination is to interpret them in a physical sense: if we can endure until the end when Jesus returns at the Rapture, then we will be saved from the persecution once and for all.

During this time of persecution, when the Antichrist rules, we will be offered a choice. Those who have been delivered to the authorities must either accept the mark of the beast and denounce the Christian faith or face affliction and death. Jesus calls on us to endure. Jesus tells us, "In your patience possess ye your souls" (Luke 21:19).

The rule of the Antichrist is explained in greater detail in Revelation 13:

> And I stood upon the sand of the sea, and saw a beast rise up out of the sea, having seven heads and ten horns, and upon his horns ten crowns, and upon his heads the name of blasphemy. And they worshipped the dragon which gave power unto the beast: and they worshipped the beast, saying, Who is like unto the beast? who is able to make war with him? And it was given unto him to make war with the saints, and to overcome them: and power was given him over all kindreds, and tongues, and nations. And all that dwell upon the earth shall worship him, whose names are not written in the book of life of the Lamb slain from the foundation of the world. If any man have an ear, let him hear. And he causeth all, both small and great, rich and poor, free and bond, to receive a mark in their right hand, or in their foreheads: and that no man might buy or sell, save he that had the mark, or the name of the beast, or the number of his name. Here is wisdom. Let him that hath understanding count the number of the beast: for it is the number of a man; and his number is Six hundred threescore and six.

The Antichrist and his false prophet make war with the saints and overcome them. God Almighty gives him power to rule over all kindreds, tongues, and nations. Great wonders and miracles are performed. Ultimately, the Antichrist causes all, both small and great, rich and poor, free and bond, to receive a mark in their right hands or in their foreheads. Without it, individuals will not be able to buy or sell or participate in normal economic activity. This mark will be required to live a normal life within society.

THE BELIEVER'S CHOICE

The persecution of the saints and the mark of the Beast tie directly to Revelation 14, where the choice between the mark of the Beast and God is presented. The result of accepting the mark of the Beast is very plain: those who take the mark are condemned to the lake of fire.

> And the third angel followed them, saying with a loud voice, If any man worship the beast and his image, and receive his mark in his forehead, or in his hand, the same shall drink of the wine of the wrath of God, which is poured out without mixture into the cup of his indignation; and he shall be tormented with fire and brimstone in the presence of the holy angels, and in the presence of the Lamb: and the smoke of their torment ascendeth up for ever and ever: and they have no rest day nor night, who worship the beast and his image, and whosoever receiveth the mark of his name. (Rev. 14:9–11)

As Jesus predicts, the persecution of the church and the believers will be great. Even today, we all must make an individual choice to believe in the God of the Bible or ignore him. In Western society, this choice is often a private decision that can be internalized. In the end times, the choice will be visible and known to all, because you will either have the mark of the Beast on your hand or forehead, or you will be cast out of society. Your choice will be plainly seen. If you try to rationalize and justify taking the mark of the Beast in order to save your life or the lives of your family, God has clearly detailed the implications of your choice.

> Whosoever shall seek to save his life shall lose it; and whosoever shall lose his life shall preserve it. (Luke 17:33)

The Bible gives us clear teachings and warnings for a reason: if you become confused, or do not recognize the end-times events and the mark for what they are, you could be deceived right into hell. Anyone who tries to rationalize the worship of the Beast or the acceptance of his mark in order to save his or her life will actually lose it. Remember that Jesus opened his remarks on the last days with the command, "Take heed that ye be not deceived." Your choice will be to either accept the mark of the Beast and condemn yourself or reject the mark and face the potentially severe earthly consequences.

In the face of personal persecution, you will need to have the patience (that is, the endurance) of the saints. In patience, we will need to possess our souls. Those who maintain their faith will be rewarded.

> Here is the patience of the saints: here are they that keep the commandments of God, and the faith of Jesus. And I heard a voice from heaven saying unto me, Write, Blessed are the dead which die in the Lord from henceforth: Yea, saith the Spirit, that they may rest from their labours; and their works do follow them. (Rev. 14:12–13)

Revelation describes those who have died in the Lord, after the Antichrist forces society to take the mark of the Beast, as *blessed*. If you die in the Lord, you will rest from your labors, and your works will follow you. This is a beautiful, powerful promise.

THE CRUX OF THE MATTER

The primary reason the doctrine of the rapture is of paramount importance is because of the persecution that will come upon the church. We *must* train Christians to be aware that this persecution could be in their futures and that they must be willing to choose the love of Christ above the love of their own lives. If they forsake Christ and follow the world into the worship of the Antichrist, their eternal souls will be at stake. The choice during these tribulation times will not be easy, but we must be willing to believe that God is real, that his Word is true, and that we must offer our lives in service to him. If you *really* believe in God, then there is no other logical choice.

I often relate the decision to believe God and follow his commandments to delayed gratification—the ability to pass by an immediate reward in order to gain a more significant one later. During my life, I have maintained financial discipline using delayed gratification. It would have been nice to own a new car when I was eighteen, but I could not afford it. So I drove old cars around for years until I could afford a new car. This allowed me to stay out of debt and avoid high interest charges that would have drained my future earnings.

The same principle applies to the spiritual. Today, I enjoy the benefits of worshiping and following a true and living God, but the real payback will not happen until much later. If I maintain discipline in my spiritual walk with God now, in the future I will realize the results of this discipline. In the face of persecution, I will be able to keep the long-term goal in focus. Don't settle for immediate gratification. If you believe God, and you face persecution, you must learn to suffer through the immediate in order to realize the long-term reward.

The call to suffering, trouble, and persecution for the sake of Jesus Christ is not new. In the last days it will be extreme, but God says that he will pay back those who trouble us:

> Seeing it is a righteous thing with God to recompense tribulation to them that trouble you; and to you who are troubled *rest with us,* when the Lord Jesus shall be revealed from heaven with his mighty angels. (2 Thess. 1:6–7, emphasis mine)

God tells us to *rest* with the saints. The call to rest here is the same call God explains in the fifth seal in Revelation 6:

> And when he had opened the fifth seal, I saw under the altar the souls of them that were slain for the word of God, and for the testimony which they held: and they cried with a loud voice, saying, How long, O Lord, holy and true, dost thou not judge and avenge our blood on them that dwell on the earth? And white robes were given unto every one of them; and it was said unto them, that they should *rest* yet for a little season, until their fellowservants also and

their brethren, that should be killed as they were, should be fulfilled. (Rev. 6:9–11)

The fifth seal describes martyrs who were slain for the Word of God and the testimony they held. The martyrs are calling out to God for justice. God answers them by providing white robes and asking them to rest for a little season, because there are more martyrs on the way. Notice that the Bible describes more fellow servants and more brethren who will be killed on the earth. Daniel further explains our relationship with the Antichrist during these difficult times:

> I beheld, and the same horn made *war with the saints*, and *prevailed against them; until* the Ancient of days came, and judgment was given to the saints of the most High; and the time came that the saints possessed the kingdom. Thus he said, The fourth beast shall be the fourth kingdom upon earth, which shall be diverse from all kingdoms, and shall devour the whole earth, and shall tread it down, and break it in pieces. And the ten horns out of this kingdom are ten kings that shall arise: and another shall rise after them; and he shall be diverse from the first, and he shall subdue three kings. And he shall speak great words against the most High, and shall *wear out the saints of the most high*, and think to change times and laws: and they shall be given into his hand until a time and times and the dividing of time. But the judgment shall sit, and they shall take away his dominion, to consume and to destroy it unto the end. (Dan. 7:21–26, emphasis mine)

I have heard preachers proclaim, "I have read the end of the book, and we win." While this statement is true for the very end, the earthly or physical end of believers in the end times will be very different. Daniel clearly states that the Antichrist will make war with the saints and that he will prevail against us. In an earthly sense, the Antichrist wins. Daniel 7:25 describes how the Antichrist will "wear out the saints of the most High." The persecution of the believer will not result in any earthly victory. We will be trampled down. We will be worn out. We will lose our lives, our families, our friends, our freedom, our ability to buy and sell. We will lose it all. But in the end, God promises that he will come and provide the victory (Daniel 7:22), and the time will come when the saints will possess the kingdom. But that should not cause us to forget that for many believers during the tribulation period, pain, betrayal, incarceration, and death will come first.

But Won't God Save Us from Persecution?

I've heard some proclaim that God would not allow the church to go through the Great Tribulation and persecution. If you recall, one pretribulation rapture enthusiast would call me a "church hater" for suggesting that we could face persecution at the hand of Antichrist. But if you also think I'm a misanthrope for proclaiming this, then I invite you to take a closer look at the Bible, at history, and even at the non-Western world around us today. There are no Scriptures that claim God will save his church or his people from persecution and hard times. Rather, multiple verses tell us we should expect persecution and tribulation:

> And ye shall be hated of all men for my name's sake: but he that endureth to the end shall be saved. (Matt. 10:22)

> And ye shall be hated of all men for my name's sake: but he that shall endure unto the end, the same shall be saved. (Mark 13:13)

> If the world hate you, ye know that it hated me before it hated you. (John 15:18)

> Marvel not, my brethren, if the world hate you. (1 John 3:13)

Moreover, the Bible is filled with examples of true believers facing persecution. Consider the exodus of Israel from Egypt. The Israelites did not just miraculously leave one day for the Promised Land—instead, Egypt began killing their male children in order to control the Jewish population. This was followed by increasing cruelty from Pharaoh and the taskmasters.

Israel witnessed the ten plagues that destroyed Egypt, but then subsequently wandered through the wilderness for forty years before they waged war to claim the Promised Land. Or take David: this future Jewish king was anointed by Samuel and promised the kingdom by God at an early age. Yet, David faced persecution at the hand of Saul for many years and had to patiently wait for the kingdom.

The theme goes on and on. Nebuchadnezzar threw three Israelite boys into a fiery furnace for not worshiping his golden statue. Daniel was persecuted and thrown into the lions' den. Elijah spent years on the run from Ahab and Jezebel. Jeremiah was considered a traitor and spent time in a dungeon, living under constant ridicule and fear of death. Nehemiah and Ezra faced persecution for rebuilding the temple and the wall of Jerusalem. Samson had his eyes plucked out by the Philistines. Ezekiel's wife died so that God could use Ezekiel's response to her death as an example of what he was trying to teach his people. Job's entire family and fortune were wiped out, and his health was taken away. John the Baptist was beheaded. The early church was heavily persecuted, and they scattered away from Jerusalem because of it. Most of the disciples became martyrs. Paul was imprisoned, stoned and left for dead, shipwrecked, and beaten. Stephen was stoned to death.

During modern times, six million Jews died in the Holocaust. In China, the Middle East, and many other parts of the world today, Christians face estrangement, imprisonment, and even death for their faith.

> And what shall I more say? for the time would fail me to tell of Gedeon, and of Barak, and of Samson, and of Jephthae; of David also, and Samuel, and of the prophets: who through faith subdued kingdoms, wrought righteousness, obtained promises, stopped the mouths of lions. Quenched the violence of fire, escaped the edge of the sword, out of weakness were made strong, waxed valiant in fight, turned to flight the armies of the aliens. Women received their dead raised to life again: and others were tortured, not accepting deliverance; that they might obtain a better resurrection: and others had trial of cruel mockings and scourgings, yea, moreover

of bonds and imprisonment: they were stoned, they were sawn asunder, were tempted, were slain with the sword: they wandered about in sheepskins and goatskins; being destitute, afflicted, tormented; (of whom the world was not worthy:) they wandered in deserts, and in mountains, and in dens and caves of the earth. (Heb. 11:32–38)

I think the point is clear. God has a different view of persecution and death than we do. Psalm 116:15 says, "Precious in the sight of the LORD is the death of his saints." Death is not the end, it is a beginning. The Bible teaches that God purifies his people through trials. Daniel 12:9–10 says, "Go your way, Daniel, for the words are shut up and sealed until the time of the end. Many shall purify themselves and make themselves white and be refined, but the wicked shall act wickedly." Revelation 21:7–8 says, "He that overcometh shall inherit these things; and I will be his God, and he shall be my son." Jesus said in Mark 10:29–30, "Verily I say unto you, there is no man that hath left house, or brethren, or sisters, or father, or mother, or wife, or children, or lands, for my sake, and the gospel's, but he shall receive an *hundredfold now* in this time…*with persecutions;* and in the world to come eternal life" (emphasis mine).

It's nice to believe that we could escape persecution, and if we do, we should thank God for his mercy. But it is not biblical to teach that we will escape and then try to proclaim the pretribulation rapture as the vehicle of that escape. In reality, such an attitude does not even recognize the present circumstances faced by many of our brothers and sisters in the world. While we are sheltered in America by our freedom of religion, persecution of believers is occurring all across the world right now.

In a Fox News article dated July 13, 2011, "Iranian Pastor Sentenced to Death Could be Executed if He Doesn't Recant, Says Verdict," an Iranian gentleman named Ghaemi reports, "Most churches in Iran operate with some degree of secrecy. They operate in homes. People take their batteries out of their cellphones and leave them at the door. They show up at random times so as to avoid the appearance of a crowd filing in. The current government sees them as a threat."

People with Bibles also appear to scare the government of China. *The Wall Street Journal* printed an article called "Beijing's Theology of Repression" in July 2011. Here are a few excerpts:

> ...the anguish of the church members at their continued intimidation by the authorities...Hundreds have been detained for short periods and the entire church leadership has been under house arrest since April...The recent crackdown on house-church Christians is the outgrowth of a Communist Party initiative launched last December, called "Operation Deterrence," to force all house-church Christians to be incorporated with the TSPM or suffer persecution...China is cracking down on Christians who consider God, not the Communist Party, the head of the church...The crackdown on Christians is part of a rising tide of repression against dissent that's often accompanied by interrogations and torture.

Based on biblical and modern examples, can we really claim God will not allow his children to go through a part of the Great Tribulation and face severe persecution because "God wouldn't do that"? I'm thankful God has allowed America to protect my religious freedom, but I cannot expect that to continue forever. Nor can I expect God will rapture me away if the liberties we currently enjoy in America start to falter. A healthy church teaches that persecution is a natural part of following God and should be expected.

Desire for the Day

Another key to the persecution during the end times is detailed in Luke 17:20–24. In these verses, Jesus briefly discusses the kingdom of God and his return in the Rapture.

> And when he was demanded of the Pharisees, when the kingdom of God should come, he answered them and said, The kingdom of God cometh not with observation: neither shall they say, Lo here! or, lo there! for, behold, the kingdom of God is within you. And

he said unto the disciples, The days will come, when ye shall desire to see one of the days of the Son of man, and ye shall not see it. And they shall say to you, See here; or, see there: go not after them, nor follow them. For as the lightning, that lighteneth out of the one part under heaven, shineth unto the other part under heaven; so shall also the Son of man be in his day. (Luke 17:20–24)

Verse 22 is fascinating. During the time of persecution, Jesus' words here will become absolutely true: "The days will come, when ye shall desire to see one of the days of the Son of man, and ye shall not see it." Due to the circumstances surrounding us, we will have a strong desire for the return of Christ in order to save us. In our minds, the Rapture will not arrive fast enough! However, we must continue to heed the call to endure until the end.

Luke 17:23 also provides another warning to avoid deception. Since the desire to see the return of the Son of Man will be so great, some may be led away by claims that Jesus can be found on the earth. We are to avoid falling prey to this deception. The reason we will know that Jesus is not on the earth is that his return will be marked by lightning across the skies of the entire earth, and he will gather his saints to him. *This cannot be missed.* We do not need to go looking for him; Jesus will come for us. Therefore, until you see Jesus return in the sky with lightning and angels and trumpets, you can rest assured that he has not returned at all. Do not be deceived by any other claims, no matter how probable, logical, or desirable.

The Bible teaches we must have the patience of the saints and not waver in our beliefs. We must comfort and edify one another. No matter how bad things may get, victory is soon to come.

Wherefore comfort yourselves together, and edify one another, even as also ye do.—(1 Thessalonians 5:11)

Chapter 7

THE SIXTH SIGN: THE ANTICHRIST IS PROCLAIMED GOD AND THE STRONG DELUSION

As Jesus continues to document the signs preceding his return, he does not use the words "and then" at this point. Rather, he uses the word "when." This seems to indicate that the persecution (fifth sign) and the abomination of desolation (sixth sign) coincide with one another. The events are not separated by time, but rather happen at the same time. Once the Antichrist is proclaimed God, dissidents will be hunted and destroyed.

This next Scripture provides direction concerning what we should do when the Antichrist is proclaimed God. We must flee. Matthew and Luke localize this advice to Jerusalem and Judea; depending on how the actual events unfold, the rest of us across the globe may decide to take it as well.

THE SIXTH SIGN: THE ABOMINATION OF DESOLATION

Matthew 24:15–20	Luke 21:20–24	Mark 13:14–18
When *ye therefore shall see the abomination of desolation, spoken of by Daniel the prophet, stand in the holy place, (whoso readeth, let him understand:) Then let them which be in Judaea flee into the mountains: Let*	*And* when *ye shall see Jerusalem compassed with armies, then know that the desolation thereof is nigh. Then let them which are in Judaea flee to the mountains; and let them which are in the countries enter thereinto. For these be the days of*	*But when ye shall see the abomination of desolation, spoken of by Daniel the prophet, standing where it ought not, (let them that readeth understand,) then let them that be in Judaea flee to the mountains: And let him that is on the housetop not go down*

Matthew 24:15–20	Luke 21:20–24	Mark 13:14–18
him which is on the housetop not come down to take any thing out of his house: Neither let him which is in the field return back to take his clothes. And woe unto them that are with child, and to them that give suck in those days! But pray ye that your flight be not in the winter, neither on the sabbath day.	*vengance, that all things which are written may be fulfilled. But woe unto them that are with child, and to them that give suck, in those days! for there shall be great distress in the land, and wrath upon this people. And they shall fall by the edge of the sword, and shall be led away captive captive into all nations: and Jerusalem shall be trodden down of the Gentiles, until the times of the Gentiles be fulfilled.*	*into the house, neither enter therein, to take any thing out of his house: And let him that is in the field not turn back again for to take up his garment. But woe to them that are with child, and to them that give suck in those days! And pray ye that your flight be not in the winter.*

The abomination of desolation, mentioned here by Jesus, was first predicted by Daniel:

And he shall confirm the covenant with many for one week: and in the midst of the week he shall cause the sacrifice and the oblation to cease, and for the overspreading of abominations he shall make it desolate, even until the consummation, and that determined shall be poured upon the desolate. (Dan. 9:27)

The Bible is *very* clear that the abomination of desolation must occur before the Rapture. To teach otherwise produces all kinds of doctrinal problems. The church *will* see the Antichrist. Proponents of the pretribulation rapture doctrine teach that Jesus could return anytime, even today. But that is not true. The Antichrist will be revealed before the return of Christ. This is very plainly stated in 2 Thessalonians 2. This Scripture is a key component of end-times doctrine that cannot be ignored. In order to explain it in further detail, let's review each of the verses individually.

> Now we beseech you, brethren, by the coming of our Lord Jesus Christ, and by our gathering together unto him…(2 Thess. 2:1)

This verse clearly describes the Rapture. Two other Scriptures, Matthew 24:31 and Mark 13:26, describe the return of Jesus as a gathering of his saints to him.

> …that ye be not soon shaken in mind, or be troubled, neither by spirit, nor by word, nor by letter as from us, as that the day of Christ is at hand. (2 Thess. 2:2)

God again calls us to endure as the day of Christ draws close. We are told not to be shaken in our minds. We are told not to be troubled in our spirits, or by words, or by letters from the saints. We must endure.

> Let no man deceive you by any means. (2 Thess. 2:3a)

Once again, we are warned against deception. We must not be deceived by any means. We must believe that the Scripture is true. Deception and the return of Christ are constantly tied together in the Scriptures. We can see this connection even in our own day; I believe that many have already been deceived into believing that the Rapture occurs prior to the great tribulation period, which is a direct contradiction of the next Scripture passage. Look at the remainder of verses 3 and 4:

> …for that day *shall not come,* except there come a falling away *first,* and that man of sin be revealed, the son of perdition; who opposeth and exalteth himself above all that is called God, or that

is worshipped; so that he as God sitteth in the temple of God, shewing himself that he is God. (2 Thess. 2:3b–4, emphasis mine)

Once again, the Scripture here ties directly into the gospel accounts. The Scripture very specifically states that the Rapture (i.e. the "coming of our Lord Jesus Christ" in 2 Thessalonians 2:1) cannot occur until there is a falling away first and the Antichrist is revealed. Second Thessalonians 2:4 also describes the abomination of desolation detailed in the Gospels as well as in Daniel. The Antichrist comes and proclaims himself as God and defiles the temple. Christ will not return until this has happened. To teach otherwise contradicts what the Scripture so plainly states.

> Remember ye not, that, when I was yet with you, I told you these things? And now ye know what withholdeth that he might be revealed in his time. (2 Thess. 2:5–6)

This last sentence describes the sovereignty of God. The only reason the Antichrist's rise has not happened already is that God has not allowed it to happen. God is controlling the timing of this event, and it will happen in God's appointed time. Even in the end of days, when all hope will appear to be lost, we must remember that God is in control of it all.

> For the mystery of iniquity doth already work: only he who now letteth will let, until he be taken out of the way. (2 Thess. 2:7)

When the time is right, God will remove the barrier that keeps evil from breaking out and manifesting itself with all power and signs and lying wonders. God will allow "that Wicked" to be revealed. Some teach that the words "until he be taken out of the way" refer to the removal of the Holy Ghost from the earth. The logic flows that if the Holy Ghost is removed, the church would need to be removed, which in turn means the Rapture must happen prior to the coming of Antichrist. This logic is flawed and cannot be supported in light of other Scripture (Mark 13:11, for example: "But when they shall lead you, and deliver you up, take no thought beforehand what ye shall speak, neither do ye premeditate: but whatsoever shall be given you in that hour, that speak ye: for it is not ye that speak, but the Holy Ghost").

"Only he who now letteth will let, until he be taken out of the way" should be taken at face value as pointing to the control and sovereignty of God in these matters. God will allow the Antichrist's abomination to happen, or it would never happen. Satan is not in charge here; he is only given power for a time.

The Antichrist and the Strong Delusion

The next section of 2 Thessalonians 2 requires a lengthy explanation. This section discusses the Antichrist and the strong delusion from God that is sent out into the world.

> And then shall that Wicked be revealed, whom the Lord shall consume with the spirit of his mouth, and shall destroy with the brightness of his coming: even him, whose coming is after the working of Satan with all power and signs and lying wonders, and with all deceivableness of unrighteousness in them that perish; because they received not the love of the truth, that they might be saved. And for this cause God shall send them strong delusion, that they should believe a lie: that they all might be damned who believed not the truth, but had pleasure in unrighteousness. (2 Thess. 2:8–12)

These verses fit right in line with the gospel accounts of the signs of the end times. The church will be persecuted. The Antichrist will proclaim himself as God. If Christians have not successfully fled into hiding, they will be delivered into persecution, prison, and death. The world will have little tolerance for the Christian (much like we see today in Iran and China). To the eyes of the deceived world, the Christian will appear to be blindly rejecting God. The Antichrist will not only claim to be God, he will have the miracles to prove it. Matthew 24:24 states, "For there shall arise false Christs, and false prophets, and shall shew great signs and wonders; insomuch that, if it were possible, they shall *deceive the very elect*" (emphasis mine). This will be a time of great doubt and deception.

However, this Scripture again points out God's sovereignty. God is in control, even of these events. Psalm 115:3 says, "But our God is in the heavens: he hath done whatsoever he hath pleased." God will accomplish his will. He does whatever he pleases. Here in 2 Thessalonians, God sends a strong delusion so that the people of earth will believe a lie, echoing the prophecies of Isaiah and Jesus:

> Make the heart of this people fat, and make their ears heavy, and shut their eyes; lest they see with their eyes, and hear with their ears, and understand with their heart, and convert, and be healed. (Isa.6:10)

> For this people's heart is waxed gross, and their ears are dull of hearing, and their eyes they have closed; lest at any time they should see with their eyes and hear with their ears, and should understand with their heart, and should be converted, and I should heal them. (Matt. 13:15)

Much could be said of this strong delusion. Today, the establishment of a one-world religion seems impossible. The major religions of the world appear to hold to completely separate belief systems with differences that cannot be resolved. It is nearly impossible to believe that the entire world will forsake its Christian, Islamic, Buddhist, Hindu, or fringe belief systems and cultures for the Antichrist. How will one individual, even with great signs and wonders, convince all the world religions that he is God and that they should worship him as God?

The answer is quite simple.

Every major religion believes that it is the one true religion and path to God. Yet, in our Western Christian culture, we hear many complain that it is hard to believe that all those other religions are wrong and that billions of people who don't accept Christ as Lord and Savior are destined to hell. We see bumper stickers using the symbols of many different religions and cults to spell out the word "coexist." The ending of the television series *Lost* took place in what looked like a typical Catholic church. However, if you looked at the props in the scene, you would notice that the stained-glass window contained all of the religious symbols in the "coexist" sign. There were also Buddist and other Eastern religious artifacts in the room.

In America, we are being fed the idea through multiple media outlets that all religions can coexist and that all paths lead to God. And herein lies a simple answer to the problem of the strong delusion.

When the Antichrist proclaims himself as God, I believe he will use the following lie or a variation of it: The Antichrist will claim he is the messiah and that he has been to earth many times before. In each of the previous visits, he will claim, the messiah presented himself to a particular culture in a concept they were familiar with and could understand and accept in order that they might accept God. God, the Antichrist may claim, was fulfilling the Christian Scripture: "To the weak became I as weak, that I might gain the weak: I am made all things to all men, that I might by all means save some" (1 Cor. 9:22). For example, the Muslims were a warrior people, so god came as Mohammed to bring the Arab nations to himself. The Asian culture was full of wisdom, so he came as Buddha to bring enlightenment. The Indian culture was full of superstition, so he came in multiple forms as many gods. The Jewish people provided blood sacrifices to God, so he came as Jesus to provide the Jews with a blood sacrifice.

The Antichrist may claim that since the world has become a smaller place through technology, and since all the cultures of the earth are beginning to blend together into one, God has returned as the final messiah one last time to bring all people and all nations together under a single worldwide rule, establishing peace on the earth. All the fighting, disagreements, and wars that have resulted from religious tensions over the centuries can now cease. There will be a new era of peace and understanding. Everyone will be brought together, because *none of the religions were wrong.* Each of them was right for its culture, its people, and its place in history. Now the messiah has returned for the final time to bring the entire world together in peace and harmony and the worship of the one true God.

That makes for a great lie, doesn't it? It is very pleasing to the ear and would be easy for people to accept—even Christians don't like to think of people burning in hell! We all want deliverance and salvation, but we want it our way, not the way of the cross of Christ. Truly, this is a strong delusion.

However, the Antichrist will still want to destroy the Jews. How will he manage to exclude them from the rest of the religions of the world? Well, he might be able to turn his followers against the Jews by using history and the Bible against them.

Think about how this might work. Of all the cultures in history, every single culture has accepted its "messiah" except one, the Jews. The Jews rejected Jesus as Messiah early in the first century. Pockets of anti-Semitism today still exist based on the notion that "the Jews killed Jesus." The Jews will again resist the Antichrist because he proclaims himself as God and sits in the temple of God showing himself that he is God (2 Thess. 2:4). Meanwhile, the Antichrist will have all the historical proof he needs to turn the world against the Jews. He could easily claim they are a stubborn and evil people who consistently reject God. He could use the entire Old Testament history of the Jews and their continual rejection of God, recorded in Scripture, to prove they cannot coexist with the rest of the world.

Consider all the Scripture references in the Old Testament that announce God's extreme displeasure with the Jews for their continued rejection of him and his commandments. We could list a multitude of references from Isaiah, Jeremiah, Ezekiel, and many of the minor prophets to "prove" this (overlooking, of course, the many, many verses that proclaim God's undying love and faithfulness toward the Jewish people). If the world believes the Antichrist is God himself, the Antichrist will be able to use the Old Testament Scriptures and references to the destruction of the Jews and their nation as the authority by which to persecute the Jews. For example, the Antichrist could easily use this Scripture as authorization to kill the Jews:

> Son of man, the house of Israel is to me become dross: all they are brass, and tin, and iron, and lead, in the midst of the furnace; they

are even the dross of silver. Therefore thus saith the Lord GOD; Because ye are all become dross, behold, therefore I will gather you into the midst of Jerusalem. As they gather silver, and brass, and iron, and lead, and tin, into the midst of the furnace, to blow the fire upon it, to melt it; so will I gather you in mine anger and in my fury, and I will leave you there, and melt you. Yea, I will gather you, and blow upon you in the fire of my wrath, and ye shall be melted in the midst thereof. As silver is melted in the midst of the furnace, so shall ye be melted in the midst thereof; and ye shall know *that I the LORD have poured out my fury upon you.* (Ezek. 22:18–22, emphasis mine)

If the Antichrist uses this logic, it seems reasonable to believe that he will be able to begin his persecution of Israel with full support of his followers. With the classic tactic of deception—mixing truth with error—he will be able to use the Bible itself as his authorization. The battle lines will be drawn, and the Antichrist could quite easily convince the world's population that they have two enemies: the Jews and the true saints of God who believe the Bible and recognize that the Antichrist is a false messiah. The Jews will be the enemy because they are Jewish. The Christians will be the enemy because they reject the Antichrist and refuse to bow to him. The Antichrist could tell the world that the only way to achieve true and lasting peace and usher in the kingdom of God will be to destroy the evil in their midst—the Jews and the Christians who will not submit to the returned messiah. Daniel 8:25 records, "And through his policy also he shall cause craft to prosper in his hand; and he shall magnify himself in his heart, *and by peace shall destroy many:* he shall also stand up against the Prince of princes; but he shall be broken without hand" (emphasis mine).

Furthermore, the Antichrist will turn the concept of good versus evil on its head. The Antichrist will claim to be God. In turn, he will claim that all the bad events happening in the world are because of Satan. The Antichrist could use the Christian Scripture from Revelation 12 to claim Satan and his followers are responsible for the world's problems:

Therefore rejoice, ye heavens, and ye that dwell in them. Woe to the inhabiters of the earth and of the sea! for the devil is come down unto you, having great wrath, because he knoweth that he hath but a short time. (Rev. 12:12)

The Antichrist could convince the world that they are fighting against the forces of evil. The Jews and real Christians will be the targets, and he will make war with them. The Antichrist will have totally flipped the tables. The world will believe they are fighting for God, not against God. They will believe they are fighting against evil, when in fact they will be fighting for evil. Jesus' words in John will become true:

They shall put you out of the synagogues: yea, the time cometh, that whosoever killeth you will think that he *doeth God service.* (John 16:2, emphasis mine)

This truly would be a strong delusion! Of course, much of this has been my own conjecture—the way I can picture the deception playing out based on the current state of the world. Satan is the master deceiver, so even if he doesn't use this tactic, there will be one just as devious. And it certainly seems that the stage is being set for something like this. There is a growing desire in our society for religious inclusion. If you read into the underpinnings of current events, it appears the nations are growing tired of the wars and religious conflicts with Muslim nations. We are tired of terrorism.

If a strong delusion like the one outlined here is accepted by the people of the world, evangelism will die. Apart from direct intervention by the Holy Ghost in the mind of a man, it will be impossible to convince anyone that Jesus Christ is the only true God and Messiah, the only way, the only truth, and the only life. The world will be worshiping the Antichrist (the Beast) and they will think they are doing God a service by persecuting Jews and Christians. Even the person sitting next to you in church each week, if he has little understanding of the Scripture and the true timing of the Rapture, could be deceived.

Signs and Wonders

In addition to the persuasive lie concerning his identity, the Antichrist will have the signs and wonders to back up his claim that he is God:

> And I saw one of his heads as it were wounded to death; and his deadly wound was healed: and all the world wondered after the beast. And they worshipped the dragon which gave power unto the beast: and they worshipped the beast, saying, Who is like unto the beast? who is able to make war with him? And there was given unto him a mouth speaking great things and blasphemies; and power was given unto him to continue forty and two months. And he opened his mouth in blasphemy against God, to blaspheme his name, and his tabernacle, and them that dwell in heaven. And it was given unto him to make war with the saints, and to overcome them: and power was given him over all kindreds, and tongues, and nations. And all that dwell upon the earth shall worship him, whose names are not written in the book of life of the Lamb slain from the foundation of the world. If any man have an ear, let him hear. He that leadeth into captivity shall go into captivity: he that killeth with the sword must be killed with the sword. Here is the patience and the faith of the saints.
>
> And I beheld another beast coming up out of the earth; and he had two horns like a lamb, and he spake as a dragon. And he exerciseth all the power of the first beast before him, and causeth the earth and them which dwell therein to worship the first beast, whose deadly wound was healed. And he doeth great wonders, so that he maketh fire come down from heaven on the earth in the sight of men, and deceiveth them that dwell on the earth by the means of those miracles which he had power to do in the sight of the beast; saying to them that dwell on the earth, that they should make an image to the beast, which had the wound by a sword, and did live.
>
> And he had power to give life unto the image of the beast, that the image of the beast should both speak, and cause that as many

as would not worship the image of the beast should be killed. And he causeth all, both small and great, rich and poor, free and bond, to receive a mark in their right hand, or in their foreheads: and that no man might buy or sell, save he that had the mark, or the name of the beast, or the number of his name. Here is wisdom. Let him that hath understanding count the number of the beast: for it is the number of a man; and his number is Six hundred threescore and six. (Rev. 13:3–18)

Revelation 13 describes the power given to the Antichrist. First, he will be wounded to death and then have a miraculous resurrection (a deliberate parody of Jesus). He is a great speaker and very charismatic. People will worship him as God. The Antichrist has a right-hand man whom the Bible later calls "the false prophet." The false prophet does great wonders and miracles and will be able to call fire down from heaven. He causes an image to be made of the Antichrist and then gives power to the image to speak. He institutes the mark of the Beast so that no commerce can occur without it. The Antichrist will be a leader full of power and signs. The world will follow.

If you don't know, understand, or believe the truth of God as documented in the Bible, then how could you resist?

Confusion of Face

The Bible describes the mental upside down of good and evil as "confusion of face" (Ezra 9:7, Dan. 9:7–8). The idea that people can become confused and assign God's attributes to a false god is nothing new.

After the destruction of Jerusalem by Nebuchadnezzar, a small remnant of Jews consulted Jeremiah on what they should do next. Their main question was whether to stay in the land of Judah or migrate to Egypt. They approached Jeremiah and made a proclamation that they would do whatever God told them to do via Jeremiah, the prophet of the Lord.

Then all the captains of the forces, and Johanan the son of Kareah, and Jezaniah the son of Hoshaiah, and all the people from the least even unto the greatest, came near, and said unto Jeremiah the prophet, Let, we beseech thee, our supplication be accepted before thee, and pray for us unto the LORD thy God, even for all this remnant; (for we are left but a few of many, as thine eyes do behold us:) that the LORD thy God may shew us the way wherein we may walk, and the thing that we may do.

Then Jeremiah the prophet said unto them, I have heard you; behold, I will pray unto the LORD your God according to your words; and it shall come to pass, that whatsoever thing the LORD shall answer you, I will declare it unto you; I will keep nothing back from you. Then they said to Jeremiah, The LORD be a true and faithful witness between us, if we do not even according to all things for the which the LORD thy God shall send thee to us. Whether it be good, or whether it be evil, we will obey the voice of the LORD our God, to whom we send thee; that it may be well with us, when we obey the voice of the LORD our God. (Jer. 42:1–6)

After ten days, the word of the Lord came to Jeremiah. God instructed his people to stay in the land of Judah and promised to bless them if they obeyed. However, the leaders and proud men did not believe the word of the Lord from Jeremiah. They called Jeremiah a liar:

And it came to pass, that when Jeremiah had made an end of speaking unto all the people all the words of the LORD their God, for which the LORD their God had sent him to them, even all these words, then spake Azariah the son of Hoshaiah, and Johanan the son of Kareah, and all the proud men, saying unto Jeremiah, Thou speakest falsely: the LORD our God hath not sent thee to say, Go not into Egypt to sojourn there: but Baruch the son of Neriah setteth thee on against us, for to deliver us into the hand of the Chaldeans, that they might put us to death, and carry us away captives into Babylon. So Johanan the son of Kareah, and all the captains of the forces, and all the people, obeyed not the voice of the LORD, to dwell in the land of Judah. (Jer. 43:1–4)

After additional discussions with the people, "confusion of face" entered the picture. The people related their bad fortune and the destruction of Judah to their failure to worship the queen of heaven properly and consistently. They believed that if they just got back to the proper worship of this pagan deity, their troubles would disappear. They were confused because they did not and could not recognize that their worship of the queen of heaven was what had provoked the Most High to anger—it was the direct *cause* of their misery.

> Then all the men which knew that their wives had burned incense unto other gods, and all the women that stood by, a great multitude, even all the people that dwelt in the land of Egypt, in Pathros, answered Jeremiah, saying, As for the word that thou hast spoken unto us in the name of the LORD, we will not hearken unto thee. But we will certainly do whatsoever thing goeth forth out of our own mouth, to burn incense unto the queen of heaven, and to pour out drink offerings unto her, as we have done, we, and our fathers, our kings, and our princes, in the cities of Judah, and in the streets of Jerusalem: for then had we plenty of victuals, and were well, and saw no evil. But since we left off to burn incense to the queen of heaven, and to pour out drink offerings unto her, we have wanted all things, and have been consumed by the sword and by the famine. And when we burned incense to the queen of heaven, and poured out drink offerings unto her, did we make her cakes to worship her, and pour out drink offerings unto her, without our men?
>
> Then Jeremiah said unto all the people, to the men, and to the women, and to all the people which had given him that answer, saying, The incense that ye burned in the cities of Judah, and in the streets of Jerusalem, ye, and your fathers, your kings, and your princes, and the people of the land, did not the LORD remember them, and came it not into his mind? So that the LORD could no longer bear, because of the evil of your doings, and because of the abominations which ye have committed; therefore is your land a desolation, and an astonishment, and a curse, without an inhabi-

tant, as at this day. Because ye have burned incense, and because ye have sinned against the Lord, and have not obeyed the voice of the Lord, nor walked in his law, nor in his statutes, nor in his testimonies; therefore this evil is happened unto you, as at this day. (Jer. 44:15–23)

Do you see the confusion exposed in this Scripture? The same could easily happen in the end times with the worship of the Antichrist. Jeremiah found it impossible to change the minds of the people, and I believe it will be equally impossible (apart from God) to change the minds of the believers in Antichrist. The Antichrist will, in their eyes, be God, and he will blame the troubles, natural disasters, and plagues on Satan—and all the time, the opposite will be true. This will be confusion of face.

The Bible has provided clear warning of things to come. The Great Tribulation will be a difficult time like no other in history. Eternal souls will hang in the balance. The call of God goes out today from our Holy Bible: Who are the true believers who will endure until the end and be saved? Who will maintain the patience of the saints, the commandments of God, and the faith of Jesus?

> To him that overcometh will I grant to sit with me in my throne, even as I also overcame, and am set down with my Father in his throne. (Rev. 3:21)

Standing Fast in the Face of Confusion

Let's turn our attention back to the remainder of 2 Thessalonians 2:

> But we are bound to give thanks alway to God for you, brethren beloved of the Lord, because God hath from the beginning chosen you to salvation through sanctification of the Spirit and belief of the truth: whereunto he called you by our gospel, to the obtaining of the glory of our Lord Jesus Christ. Therefore, brethren, stand fast, and hold the traditions which ye have been taught, whether by word, or our epistle. (2 Thess. 2:13–15)

God commands us to stand fast and hold the traditions that we have been taught. We must not waver in our faith. Regardless of the strong delusion and the events unfolding around us, we must hold fast to the traditions and believe the Bible.

> Now our Lord Jesus Christ himself, and God, even our Father, which hath loved us, and hath given us everlasting consolation and good hope through grace, comfort your hearts, and stablish you in every good word and work. (2 Thess. 2:16–17)

Here again we have God reaching out to us and telling us that he has provided everlasting consolation, good hope, and comfort. I hope you will take heart at the way this passage concludes. Even though the Bible is predicting a tough time, God reminds us of his love toward us. Even in the worst of the end times, when all hope seems lost, God Almighty will provide our consolation and hope through his grace. And if God provides consolation and good hope, we can rest assured that he will give us the strength to endure the trials and reject Antichrist.

Chapter 8

THE JEWS AND THE MARK OF THE BEAST

One aspect of the end times that needs to be addressed is the plight of the Jews during the Great Tribulation. We focus a lot on the church during the end times, but we often ignore the Jews. However, we must remember that the Jewish people are God's chosen and the apple of his eye.

> For the LORD's portion is his people; Jacob is the lot of his inheritance. He found him in a desert land, and in the waste howling wilderness; he led him about, he instructed him, he kept him as the apple of his eye. (Deut. 32:9–12)

There are many Old Testament prophecies that predict the rise of the kingdom of God with the Jews as an integral part of that kingdom. Therefore, God has a plan for protecting the Jews from the rise of Antichrist and the strong delusion that will overtake the world.

In Ezekiel 37, God shows two sticks being combined into one. God explained that one day, the split Jewish nation of Ezekiel's day would again become a single nation (Ezek. 37:15–21). This prophecy was fulfilled in 1948. However, the prophecy continues to explain that there will be one king and one shepherd over them, and God's sanctuary will be over them forever. This part of the prophecy will be fulfilled in the future.

> And I will make them one nation in the land upon the mountains of Israel; and one king shall be king to them all: and they shall be no more two nations, neither shall they be divided into two kingdoms any more at all. Neither shall they defile themselves any more with their idols, nor with their detestable things, nor with any of their transgressions: but I will save them out of all their

dwellingplaces, wherein they have sinned, and will cleanse them: so shall they be my people, and I will be their God.

And David my servant shall be king over them; and they all shall have one shepherd: they shall also walk in my judgments, and observe my statutes, and do them. And they shall dwell in the land that I have given unto Jacob my servant, wherein your fathers have dwelt; and they shall dwell therein, even they, and their children, and their children's children for ever: and my servant David shall be their prince for ever.

Moreover I will make a covenant of peace with them; it shall be an everlasting covenant with them: and I will place them, and multiply them, and will set my sanctuary in the midst of them for evermore. My tabernacle also shall be with them: yea, I will be their God, and they shall be my people. And the heathen shall know that I the LORD do sanctify Israel, when my sanctuary shall be in the midst of them for evermore. (Ezek. 37:22–28)

THE MARK, THE LAKE OF FIRE, AND THE JEWISH QUESTION

As outlined in the previous two chapters, Revelation is clear there will come a time when no man will be able to buy or sell without the mark of the Beast, and anyone who takes the mark of the Beast will be condemned to the lake of fire (Rev. 13:16–18, Rev. 14:9–11).

Most Jews during the last days will not be Christians, since the Jewish religion does not recognize Jesus Christ as the one true Messiah. However, the Jews are obviously part of the world and her economy. This presents us with a problem, because if they accept the mark of the Beast because of the strong delusion, they will be destined for hell and cannot take part in the kingdom of God—an exclusion that is clearly contrary to prophecy.

This begs a few questions that must be answered. Since the Jews do not believe in Jesus as the Messiah, how is it possible that the Jews will avoid the mark of the Beast? If participating in the world's economy on both a national and personal level requires the mark, then why wouldn't the Jews take the mark? If the entire world believes the Antichrist is the messiah, how will the Jews avoid believing the same deception?

I believe a plausible answer can be found in our history, current events, and the Scriptures. The previous chapter already looked at how the Jews will likely be excluded from the one-world peace. Likewise, the Jews will be protected from the mark of the Beast because they will be prohibited from taking the mark by the Antichrist and his governments. The Jews will be segregated and separated from the rest of society and treated as second-class citizens of the world. God will protect the Jews and their eternal souls from the Antichrist and his deception by using anti-Semitism and persecution of the Jews. The world will unite in its rejection of the Jewish people and the nation of Israel.

But God will protect his chosen people, as he allegorically describes in Revelation 12:

> And when the dragon saw that he was cast unto the earth, he persecuted the woman which brought forth the man child. And to the woman were given two wings of a great eagle, that she might fly into the wilderness, into her place, where she is nourished for a time, and times, and half a time, from the face of the serpent. And the serpent cast out of his mouth water as a flood after the woman, that he might cause her to be carried away of the flood. And the earth helped the woman, and the earth opened her mouth, and swallowed up the flood which the dragon cast out of his mouth. And the dragon was wroth with the woman, and went to make war with the remnant of her seed, which keep the commandments of God, and have the testimony of Jesus Christ. (Rev. 12:13–17)

Anti-Semitism Explosion

Anti-Semitism is nothing new. It is an age-old problem that has stretched over the millennia. The Bible records that Egypt made the Jews slaves (Exod. 1:8–14). In ancient Persia, Haman used King Ahasuerus's authority to attempt a mass slaughter of the Jews (Esther 3:8–11). The Jews faced disruption while rebuilding Jerusalem and the temple during the days of Ezra and Nehemiah (Neh. 2:10, 19; and Neh. 4:1–9). History records that the early Christian church held the Jews responsible for the death of Jesus Christ, which resulted in continual persecution of the Jews throughout the Western world. "Writings by church leaders accused the Jews of being idolaters, torturers, spiritually deaf, blasphemers, gluttons, adulterers, cannibals, Christ killers, and beyond God's forgiveness."[11]

> In 306, the Synod of Elvira prohibited intermarriage and sexual intercourse between Christians and Jews and prohibited them from eating together. In 533–541, the Council of Orleans prohibited marriages between Christians and Jews and forbade the conversion to Judaism by Christians. In 692, the Trulanic Synod prohibited Christians from being treated by Jewish doctors. In 1050, the Synod of Narbonne prohibited Christians from living in Jewish homes. In 1078, the Synod of Gerona required Jews to pay taxes to support the church. In 1179, the Third Lateran Council prohibited certain medical care to be provided by Christians to Jews. In 1215, the Fourth Lateran Council required Jews to wear special clothing to distinguish them from Christians. In 1431–1443, the Council of Basel forbade Jews to attend Universities and from acting as agents in the conclusion of contracts between Christians. It also required that they attend church sermons.[12]

In more recent history, Martin Luther of Germany accepted the Jews in his early ministry and pleaded for their salvation. But later in life, Luther wrote a few anti-Jewish rants that later haunted the Jewish people. Luther's published works vilifying the Jews became the springboard for Hitler's persecution of the Jews four hundred years later.

Luther wrote:

> What shall we Christians do with this rejected and condemned people, the Jews? I shall give you my sincere advice. First, to set fire to their synagogues or schools, and to buy and cover with dirt whatever will not burn. Second, I advise that their houses also be razed and destroyed. Third, I advise that all their prayer books and

Talmudic writings, in which such idolatry , lies, cursing, and blasphemy are taught, be taken from them. Fourth, I advise that their rabbis be forbidden to teach henceforth on pain of loss of life and limb. Fifth, I advise that safe conduct on the highways be abolished completely for the Jews. Let them stay at home. Sixth, I advise that usury be prohibited to them, and that all cash and treasures of silver and gold be taken from them and put aside for safekeeping. Seventh, I recommend putting a flail, an ax, a hoe, a spade, a distaff, or a spindle into the hands of young, strong Jews and Jewesses and letting them earn their bread in the sweat of their brow.[13]

As you probably remember from seventh-grade history class, Hitler rose in the Christian nation of Germany and used Luther's rants in support of his persecution of the Jews. The church in Germany did not object. One of the early laws passed by Hitler included the "Aryan Paragraph," which demanded that all government employees must be of Aryan stock and that anyone of Jewish descent must lose their job.[14]

From there, Hitler started removing the civil liberties of the Jewish people. At one point, Hitler declared a boycott against Jewish stores across Germany. A rally was held with signs that stated "Germans, protect yourselves! Don't buy from Jews!" and "Germans, defend yourselves from Jewish Atrocity Propaganda—buy only at German shops!"[15]

In 1933, the Nazis continued the campaign to legally bar Jews from state-affiliated institutions. On April 7, 1933, the Jews were prohibited from serving as patent lawyers. On April 22, 1933, Jewish doctors, dentists, and dental technicians were prohibited from working in institutions with state-run insurance. On April 25, 1933, Hitler placed strict limits on how many Jewish children could attend public school. On May 6, 1933, Hitler placed strict limits on how many Jews could serve as university professors, lecturers, and notaries. During the fall of 1933, the laws were extended to all spouses of non-Aryans. On September 29, 1933, the Jews were banned from all cultural and entertainment activities, including the worlds of film, theater, literature, and the arts. Shortly thereafter, Hitler placed all newspapers under Nazi control, expelling Jews from the world of journalism. Between 1933 and 1945, the Holocaust took place under Nazi control. Six million Jews were slaughtered by the Nazis. In 1948, the nation of Israel was reborn.

CURRENT EVENTS

In America, our liberties have sheltered us from the anti-Semitism that plagues the rest of the world. A large portion of the global population believes the world's problems could be solved with the removal of the nation of Israel. If this attitude continues, it is easy to imagine a world where the Jews will be cut off from the international community in an attempt to bring down the nation of Israel.

The United States Holocaust Memorial Museum reports an increase in anti-Semitism in recent years.[16]

The president of Iran mocks the idea of a Holocast and calls it a "myth." In certain Islamic countries, anti-Semitism is promoted through education, media, and politics. The hatred of Jews is showing up across the Internet. The same thing is starting to happen in America. In April 2011, it was reported that the New Black Panther Party organized a National Day of Action in forty cities. One of the goals of the organization was to oppose Jews and "Zionism."[17]

In Amsterdam on February 2011, it was reported that Jewish groups were asking the government for swift punishment for those who deny the Holocaust as a way to combat the growth in anti-Semitism. The same news story referenced another interview in which one individual thought the Jews should be "exterminated."[18]

Given our historical treatment of the Jews, as well as the rise in anti-Semitism today, the governments of the Antichrist could easily institute laws that prohibit the Jews from participating in the world's economy, much like Hitler did in Germany.

Such a prohibition might well take the form of an embargo on the nation of Israel in order to gain concessions from Israel. It also could be used as a means to simply destroy Israel without the need for warfare. And it would certainly prevent Jews from taking the mark of the Beast. In the end times, Israel and the Jews may become isolated from the international community. The only refuge from the abuses of anti-Semitism and segregation will be the sovereign nation of Israel. If you are Jewish and prohibited from taking the mark of the Beast, then you will not be able to hold a job, earn a living, or buy and sell in any other part of the world. Your only option will be to move to Israel as a means for survival. The Bible predicts a great gathering of Jews from all corners of the earth. If my guesses here prove accurate, the only place a Jew will be able to find refuge will be Israel, which will force a large influx of Jews from all over the world back to the Holy Land.

Again, while this is conjecture on my part, it fits much of what we see and have seen in the world. Numerous Scriptures paint the picture of the gathering of the Jews back to Israel:

> Since thou wast precious in my sight, thou hast been honourable, and I have loved thee: therefore will I give men for thee, and people for thy life. Fear not: for I am with thee: I will bring thy seed from the east, and gather thee from the west; I will say to the north, Give up; and to the south, Keep not back: bring my sons from far, and my daughters from the ends of the earth. (Isa. 43:4–6)

> And it shall come to pass in that day, that the Lord shall set his hand again the second time to recover the remnant of his people, which shall be left, from Assyria, and from Egypt, and from Pathros, and from Cush, and from Elam, and from Shinar, and from Hamath, and from the islands of the sea. And he shall set up an ensign for the nations, and shall assemble the outcasts of Israel, and gather together the dispersed of Judah from the four corners of the earth. (Isa. 11:11–12)

> For a small moment have I forsaken thee; but with great mercies will I gather thee. (Isa. 54:7)

> And I will gather the remnant of my flock out of all countries whither I have driven them, and will bring them again to their folds; and they shall be fruitful and increase. (Jer. 23:3)

I will gather them that are sorrowful for the solemn assembly, who are of thee, to whom the reproach of it was a burden. Behold, at that time I will undo all that afflict thee: and I will save her that halteth, and gather her that was driven out; and I will get them praise and fame in every land where they have been put to shame. At that time will I bring you again, even in the time that I gather you: for I will make you a name and a praise among all people of the earth, when I turn back your captivity before your eyes, saith the LORD. (Zeph. 3:18–20)

The Two Witnesses of Revelation 11

Assuming I'm right that the Jews will become economically suppressed and isolated in Israel, we might ask why the Beast wouldn't just destroy Israel with a few targeted nuclear bombs. The bigger picture of Scripture gives us insight on this: here is where the two witnesses of Revelation might come into play. The Antichrist will not move upon Israel because of God's supernatural protection. Revelation 12:14 says that Israel (allegorically referred to as "the woman") will be nourished for three-and-a-half years. In addition, God describes two witnesses who will prophesy for 1,260 days (three-and-a-half years):

> And I will give power unto my two witnesses, and they shall prophesy a thousand two hundred and threescore days, clothed in sackcloth. These are the two olive trees, and the two candlesticks standing before the God of the earth. And if any man will hurt them, fire proceedeth out of their mouth, and devoureth their enemies: and if any man will hurt them, he must in this manner be killed. These have power to shut heaven, that it rain not in the days of their prophecy: and have power over waters to turn them to blood, and to smite the earth with all plagues, as often as they will.
>
> And when they shall have finished their testimony, the beast that ascendeth out of the bottomless pit shall make war against them, and shall overcome them, and kill them. And their dead bodies shall lie in the street of the great city, which spiritually is

called Sodom and Egypt, where also our Lord was crucified. And they of the people and kindreds and tongues and nations shall see their dead bodies three days and an half, and shall not suffer their dead bodies to be put in graves. And they that dwell upon the earth shall rejoice over them, and make merry, and shall send gifts one to another; because these two prophets tormented them that dwelt on the earth.

And after three days and an half the spirit of life from God entered into them, and they stood upon their feet; and great fear fell upon them which saw them. And they heard a great voice from heaven saying unto them, Come up hither. And they ascended up to heaven in a cloud; and their enemies beheld them. And the same hour was there a great earthquake, and the tenth part of the city fell, and in the earthquake were slain of men seven thousand: and the remnant were affrighted, and gave glory to the God of heaven. (Rev. 11:3–13)

The two prophets will protect Israel for the three-and-a-half years. If any man attempts to hurt these prophets, he will be devoured by fire. The prophets will afflict the earth with plagues as often as they wish. No one will have the willpower to move against Israel during the days of the prophets! Even the Antichrist will be stymied.

Since man's perception of good and evil will have been turned, the world will probably view these prophets as agents of Satan. After 1,260 days, the Antichrist will kill the two prophets, and the world will rejoice. The world might believe that with the removal of the prophets, the barriers to the final destruction of the Jews and Israel have been removed. The countdown to Armageddon can begin.

And I saw three unclean spirits like frogs come out of the mouth of the dragon, and out of the mouth of the beast, and out of the mouth of the false prophet. For they are the spirits of devils, working miracles, which go forth unto the kings of the earth and of the whole world, to gather them to the battle of that great day of God

Almighty. Behold, I come as a thief. Blessed is he that watcheth, and keepeth his garments, lest he walk naked, and they see his shame. And he gathered them together into a place called in the Hebrew tongue Armageddon. (Rev. 16:13–16)

As we move toward Armageddon in our study, you may be asking why the plight of the Jews should matter so much to us. Besides the fact that our God loves the Jewish people, it matters because we could be occupants of the same boat. In the tribulation, both Christians and Jews will be oppressed by the Antichrist and his government. I believe we should always stand behind Israel and the Jewish people. After all, we might end up needing to use their country as our refuge!

Chapter 9

THE SEVENTH, EIGHTH, AND NINTH SIGNS: GREAT TRIBULATION, FALSE CHRISTS, HEAVEN AND EARTH SHAKEN

The next sign is what the Bible calls "great tribulation." It happens on the heels of the great persecution (fifth sign) and the abomination of desolation (sixth sign). As was earlier pointed out, there does not appear to be much of a separation in time between these signs. Rather, they happen together or are very closely linked. Jesus does not use the words "and then" when speaking of these events. Rather, he uses the words "for then," "and," and "for in those days." Here is how the Gospels describe the time period:

THE SEVENTH SIGN: GREAT TRIBULATION

Matthew 24:21–22	Luke 21:25–26	Mark 13:19
For then *shall be* great tribulation, *such as was* not since the beginning of the world to this time, no, nor ever shall be. *And except those days should be shortened, there should no flesh be saved: but for the elect's sake those days shall be shortened.*	And *there shall be* signs in the sun, and in the moon, and in the stars; and upon the earth distress of nations, with perplexity; the sea and the waves roaring; *Men's hearts failing them for fear, and for looking after those things which are coming on the earth: for the powers of heaven shall be shaken.*	For in those days shall be affliction, such as was not from the beginning of the creation which God created unto this time, neither shall be. *And except that the Lord had shortened those days, no flesh should be saved: but for the elect's sake, whom he hath chosen, he hath shortened the days.*

The Gospels record great tribulation and affliction in this time. Jesus said that this period will not match anything in history and will never again be repeated. Matthew and Mark do not offer any further descriptions of this time period in their accounts except to say that it will be bad. So bad, in fact, that if the time period were not short, there would be no survivors. Matthew records that the only reason God is providing any mercy and grace at all is because of the "elect" (i.e. Christians) still present on the earth.

In order to understand the events of the Great Tribulation, it helps to compare the Gospels to the Revelation. The key to this comparison lies within the gospel of Luke. Luke describes this time period in various sections instead of in a linear string of verses. The description in Luke 21:11b–12a is interrupted by a look back: "And fearful sights and great signs shall there be from heaven. But *before* all these…"

Luke 21:12a is the key: "But before all these." Jesus says that before the fearful sights and great heavenly signs, the persecution and the revealing of the Antichrist will occur, as explained in the previous chapters. Therefore, if you put Luke 21:11b together with Luke 21:25–26, the timeline starts to make sense. Look at how this reads in sequence:

> And great signs shall there be from heaven (Luke 21:11b). And there shall be signs in the sun, and in the moon, and in the stars; and upon the earth distress of nations, with perplexity; the sea and the waves roaring; men's hearts failing them for fear, and for looking after those things which are coming on the earth: for the powers of heaven shall be shaken. (Luke 21:25–26)

Now look at how closely this matches the sixth seal in Revelation 6:

> And I beheld when he had opened the sixth seal, and, lo, there was a great earthquake; and the sun became black as sackcloth of hair, and the moon became as blood; and the stars of heaven fell unto the earth, even as a fig tree casteth her untimely figs, when she is shaken of a mighty wind. And the heaven departed as a scroll when it is rolled together; and every mountain and island were moved

out of their places. And the kings of the earth, and the great men, and the rich men, and the chief captains, and the mighty men, and every bondman, and every free man, hid themselves in the dens and in the rocks of the mountains; and said to the mountains and rocks, Fall on us, and hide us from the face of him that sitteth on the throne, and from the wrath of the Lamb: for the great day of his wrath is come; and who shall be able to stand? (Rev. 6:12–17)

As part of this great tribulation, Luke records that there will be great signs in heaven. Again, Revelation and the Gospels line up perfectly. Luke says that there will be signs in the sun, while Revelation declares that the sun will become black. Luke mentions signs in the moon, while Revelation records a blood moon. Luke describes signs in the stars, while Revelation says that the stars of heaven will fall to the earth (meteor showers?). Luke says that men's hearts will fail from fear, and Revelation describes men hiding in the rocks for fear and begging for the mountains to hide them. Even after accepting the mark of the Beast and worshiping Antichrist as god, they somehow come to understand that the God of the Bible is in control.

Luke says that the sea and waves will roar, while Revelation describes a great earthquake so massive that every mountain and island is moved out of its place. The natural effects of a massive earthquake in and around islands are, of course, tsunamis (i.e. the sea and waves roaring).

Now, a skeptic might say that the Bible is taking liberties in describing an earthquake so massive that every mountain and island is moved out of its place. However, the 2011 Japanese quake and a subsequent report by NASA proves this is possible. This report calculated that the position of the Earth's figure axis should have shifted about 6.5 inches during the earthquake.[19]

I'm no scientist, but I do know that if the earth's axis moved by 6.5 inches in 2011, then every mountain and island on earth moved with it! If the earthquakes described in Revelation are severe, then the distribution of mass in the earth will change and affect the earth's axis, which will fulfill the prophecy.

Finally, Luke says that the powers of heaven will be shaken, while Revelation describes the event as the heavens departing as a scroll when it is rolled together:

LUKE	REVELATION
Great Signs in Heaven	
Signs in Sun	The sun became black as sackcloth of hair
Signs in Moon	The moon became as blood
Signs in the Stars	The stars of heaven fell unto the earth
Distress and Perplexity of Nations	The kings of the earth (nations) are distreessed
Men's Hearts Failing from Fear	All men hid themselves for fear. They are so fearful they ask the mountains and rocks to fall on them to hide them from the face of him that sitteth on the throne and from the wrath of the Lamb.
Sea and Waves Roaring	A great earthquake. Every mountain and island is moved out of its place. The natural result would be multiple tsunamis.
The Powers of Heaven Shaken	The heave departed as a scroll when it is rolled together.

This is quite a list! Everything in heaven and earth is turned on its ear. This is the great tribulation and affliction as described by Jesus in the Gospels and again in Revelation.

There Cannot Be Two Great Tribulations

If you believe in the pretribulation rapture, you might continue to be skeptical of the chronology I've presented thus far (I sympathize—it's hard to change a paradigm that's been firmly fixed in one's head!). However, I'd ask that you think about the description provided in the Gospels in relation to the timing of the Rapture.

If you claim that the signs provided by Jesus are different from the account in the Revelation (or occur at a different time), then you are forced to teach that there are two great tribulations. Your doctrine will need to include a great tribulation as described in the Gospels, the Rapture, and then the Great Tribulation as described in the Revelation. However, this creates a clear contradiction. In Matthew 24:21, Jesus says, "For *then* shall be great tribulation, such as was not since the beginning of the world to this time, no, *nor ever shall be*" (emphasis mine).

Jesus states in Matthew 24:21 that this time period is the Great Tribulation, that it cannot be compared to anything in our entire history, and that it will not be repeated again in the future. Jesus is stating that there is only one Great Tribulation.

Moreover, Jesus clearly says this will happen *before* his return and the rapture of the church. The rapture of the elect is not described until Matthew 24:27–31. Both verse 21 and verse 30 prove again that these events are in chronological order when they use the words "for then" and "and then."

> *And then* shall appear the sign of the Son of man in heaven: *and then* shall all the tribes of the earth mourn, and they shall see the Son of man coming in the clouds of heaven with power and great glory. And he shall send his angels with a great sound of a trumpet, and they shall gather together his elect from the four winds, from one end of heaven to the other. (Matt. 24:30–31, emphasis mine)

Do you see the scriptural problem that the pretribulation rapture doctrine produces here? If you believe that Jesus is describing the Rapture in Matthew 24, then you are forced to teach a chronology wherein there is great tribulation (as described in the Gospels), the Rapture, and then great tribulation (as described in Revelation).

As an alternative, you might insert the claim that Matthew 24 describes the second coming of Christ and not the Rapture. However, the second coming described in Revelation 19 does not match the return of Christ described in the Gospels. The account in Matthew includes a gathering of the saints, a trumpet, angels, lightning, and clouds (this is clearly the Rapture, but more on this later). Meanwhile, Revelation describes the second coming as Jesus Christ riding on a white horse and leading the armies of heaven, and his purpose is vengeance. Revelation 19 does not mention trumpets, nor lightning, nor clouds, nor a gathering of God's people. The second coming in Revelation in no way matches the return of Christ described in the Gospels. It appears that you must force fit the second coming into Matthew 24 in order to maintain the pretribulation rapture doctrine.

This leads to my next point. As we noted at the beginning, the disciples plainly asked Jesus for the signs of his return. If you believe that Matthew 24 refers to the second coming (and not the Rapture), then why did Jesus leave out the Rapture in its entirety when he responded? Why didn't Jesus start with something like, "I'll come back and gather my church, and then . . ." Or if you believe that Jesus will arrive as a complete surprise, then why didn't Jesus just answer the question by saying that there would be no signs? Why would Jesus take the time to explain a chronology of events if we are already raptured away prior to these events?

If you take a step back and consider the information presented, you can see that there is quite a compelling case that the church will experience the signs described by Jesus in the Gospels before the Rapture, and that the gospel accounts match the Revelation.

The Eighth Sign: False Christs and Prophets

If we look back at what has occurred so far in the timeline, you can see that the world will be in great turmoil. The unbelievers are being marked and committed to the Antichrist. The true saints of God are dead, imprisoned, or on the run. The Jews are under persecution by the Antichrist and possibly segregated from the rest of the world economy. The world itself is experiencing great tribulation.

On top of these events, if believers have accepted a false doctrine regarding the timing of a pretribulation rapture, there will be great confusion. The confusion based on wrong expectations could cause people to be swayed into believing in false Christs. Jesus provides this specific warning.

THE EIGHTH SIGN: FALSE CHRISTS AND FALSE PROPHETS

Matthew 24:23–26	Mark 13:21–23
Then if any man shall say unto you, Lo, here is Christ, or there; believe it not. For there shall arise false Christs, and false prophets, and shall shew great signs and wonders; insomuch that, if it were possible, they shall deceive the very elect. Behold, I have told you before. Wherefore if they shall say unto you, Behold, he is in the desert; go not forth: behold, he is in the secret chambers; believe it not.	*And then if any man shall say to you, Lo, here is Christ; or, lo, he is there; believe him not: For false Christs and false prophets shall rise, and shall shew signs and wonder, to seduce if it were possible, even the elect. But take ye heed: behold,* I have foretold you all things.

Jesus clearly states that the deception in the last days will be great. Since the Antichrist will be wearing out the saints of the Most High (Dan. 7:25), I suspect that many of the elect will be eager to escape and find Jesus. In Luke 17:22–23, Jesus said, "The days will come, when ye shall desire to see one of the days of the Son of man, and ye shall not see it. And they shall say to you, See here; or, see there: go not after them, nor follow them."

Since the times will be bad and the deception will be great, there will be a strong temptation to believe false Christs and their signs and wonders. Satan will attempt to seduce the elect into believing lies. Jesus repeatedly tells us to take heed against such deception.

Mark 13:23 holds a key statement. Jesus says, "Behold, I have *foretold* you *all* things" (emphasis mine). Jesus is making the statement that the signs he is providing regarding the end of the world and his return are complete.

God is not the author of confusion. Jesus is telling the saints, the elect, what to expect. There will be a lot of spiritual forces at work, and we must be able to hold fast to the Scripture so that we can endure until his return and our rapture. Jesus is warning us to maintain our faith and avoid deception, even though events will be confusing and doubt will cloud our faith. We must remain true to God regardless of the circumstances.

THE NINTH SIGN: HEAVEN AND EARTH SHAKEN—AGAIN

As we continue in the chronology of events leading to the return of Christ and the end of the world, Jesus uses the phrases "immediately after" and "after that tribulation" to describe another set of judgments. Look at the gospel accounts:

THE NINTH SIGN: HEAVEN AND EARTH SHAKEN—AGAIN

Matthew 24:29	Mark 13:24–25
Immediately after *the tribulation of those days shall the sun be darkened, and the moon shall not give her light, and the stars shall fall from heaven, and the powers of the heavens shall be shaken.*	*But in those days,* after *that tribulation, the sun shall be darkened, and the moon shall not give her light, And the stars of heaven shall fall, and the powers that are in heaven shall be shaken*

These descriptions again match the Revelation, where the trumpet judgments are described. Here is what is recorded in Revelation 8:

> The first angel sounded, and there followed hail and fire mingled with blood, and they were cast upon the earth: and the third part of trees was burnt up, and all green grass was burnt up.
>
> And the second angel sounded, and as it were a great mountain burning with fire was cast into the sea: and the third part of the sea became blood; and the third part of the creatures which were in the sea, and had life, died; and the third part of the ships were destroyed.

And the third angel sounded, and there fell a great star from heaven, burning as it were a lamp, and it fell upon the third part of the rivers, and upon the fountains of waters; and the name of the star is called Wormwood: and the third part of the waters became wormwood; and many men died of the waters, because they were made bitter.

And the fourth angel sounded, and the third part of the sun was smitten, and the third part of the moon, and the third part of the stars; so as the third part of them was darkened, and the day shone not for a third part of it, and the night likewise. And I beheld, and heard an angel flying through the midst of heaven, saying with a loud voice, Woe, woe, woe, to the inhabiters of the earth by reason of the other voices of the trumpet of the three angels, which are yet to sound! (Rev. 8:7–13)

Matthew and Mark record that the powers of heaven will be shaken, while Revelation describes the first trumpet as hail mingled with fire and blood. Revelation then describes a second trumpet where a burning mountain cast into the sea turns one-third of the ocean to blood (this is not mentioned in the Gospels). The Gospels then describe stars falling from heaven, while Revelation describes the third trumpet as a star from heaven called Wormwood that makes one third of the waters bitter. The Gospels say that the sun and moon will be darkened, while Revelation says that with the fourth trumpet, one-third of the sun and one-third of the moon will be darkened.

Matthew and Mark record the following for the Ninth Sign:	Revelation 8 records the following Trumpets:
Power of heaven shaken =	1st Trumpet=Hail, Fire, Blood, 1/2 of the trees/grass burn away
	2nd Trumpet=Burning mountain, 1/3 of the sea becomes blood
Stars from heaven =	3rd Trumpet=Star from heaven, 1/3

Sun darkened =	of the waters become bitter
	4th Trumpet=1/3 of the sun darkened
Moon darkened =	4th Trumpet=1/3 of the moon darkened
	5th Trumpet=Demonic torment of men

The gospel accounts do not mention the second, fifth, or sixth trumpet judgments, for the simple reason that these judgments will not come against believers. As the trumpet judgments unfold, there has already been a separation on the earth. The followers of Antichrist are marked.

The fifth trumpet describes demon locusts that are unleashed upon the earth. Their mission is to torment the followers of antichrist, but they are not to touch the elect:

> And the fifth angel sounded, and I saw a star fall from heaven unto the earth: and to him was given the key of the bottomless pit. And he opened the bottomless pit; and there arose a smoke out of the pit, as the smoke of a great furnace; and the sun and the air were darkened by reason of the smoke of the pit. And there came out of the smoke locusts upon the earth: and unto them was given power, as the scorpions of the earth have power. And it was commanded them that they should not hurt the grass of the earth, neither any green thing, neither any tree; but *only those men* which have *not the seal of God* in their foreheads. And to them it was given that they should not kill them, but that they should be tormented five months: and their torment was as the torment of a scorpion, when he striketh a man. And in those days shall men seek death, and shall not find it; and shall desire to die, and death shall flee from them. (Rev. 9:1–6, emphasis mine)

This terrifying passage describes the dark days of the Great Tribulation. However, for the believer in Christ, hope is just on the horizon. The return of Christ is imminent.

Chapter 10

THE TENTH SIGN: THE MYSTERY OF GOD REVEALED AT THE LAST TRUMP—THE RETURN OF JESUS CHRIST

The tenth sign. "And then" something amazing happens. After all the turmoil, and trouble, and persecution, dawn is ready to break. Salvation day has arrived.

It is difficult to imagine the emotions and euphoria that will run wild when Christ returns for his saints. This is the moment of truth. This is where all the doubts, second-guessing, fear, and pain will be wiped away. This is where you will stand with your hands held high in triumph because you maintained the faith and endured until the end. You looked past the lies and grand deceptions and clung to the truth of the Word of God. Today is payback day. And you are one of a select group of individuals who will be gathered directly into heaven for reunion with fellow believers and God himself. The days of adversity are over. Free at last, free at last, thank God Almighty, you are free at last!

THE TENTH SIGN: THE RETURN OF CHRIST AT THE RAPTURE

Matthew 24:27–31	Luke 21:27–28	Mark 13:26–27
For as the lightning cometh out of the east, and shineth even unto the west; so shall also coming of the Son of man be. For wheresoever the carcase is, there will the eagles be gathered together. And then shall appear	*And then shall they see the Son of Man coming in a cloud with power and great glory. And when these things begin to come to pass, then look up, and lift up your heads; for your*	*And then shall they see the Son of Man coming in the clouds with great power and glory. And then shall he send his angels, shall gather together his elect from the four winds, from the uttermost part of the*

Matthew 24:27–31	Luke 21:27–28	Mark 13:26–27
the sign of the Son of man in heaven: and then shall all the tribes of the earth mourn, and they shall see the Son of man coming in the clouds of heaven with power and great glory. And he shall send his angels with a great sound of a trumpet, and they shall gather together his elect from the four winds, from one end of heaven to the other.	*redemption draweth nigh.*	*earth to the uttermost part of heaven.*

THE LAST TRUMPET IS THE MYSTERY OF GOD, THE RAPTURE

The next two verses are where it all started for me. If you read the introduction of this book, you'll remember that I described a Sunday morning in church when 1 Corinthians 15:51–52 was read, which led me to another verse, and another, and so on. The next verse was Revelation 10:7. Look at these verses side-by-side.

1 Corinthians 15:51–52	Revelation 10:7
Behold, I shew you a mystery; *we shall not all sleep, but we shall all be changed. In a moment, in the twinkling of an eye, at the* last trump; *for the trumpet shall sound, and the dead shall be raised incorruptible, and we shall be changed.*	*But in the days of the voice of the seventh angel, when he shall begin to sound, the mystery of God should be finished, as he hath declared to his servants the prophets.*

Do you see the similarity? The seventh angel sounds the last trumpet. After the seventh trumpet sounds, there are no additional trumpets mentioned anywhere in the Revelation. Nowhere. Nada. The trumpets are put away. There is not a single trumpet mentioned in Revelation 19 at the second coming of Christ. The "last trumpet" as described in 1 Corinthians 15:15–52 is the same "last trumpet" described in Revelation 10:7.

Once I came to understand that these verses were describing the same event, all of the pieces began to fall into place. First Corinthians 15:51–52 and Revelation 10:7, as well as the detailed descriptions of the signs in the Gospels and the account in the Revelation, all tie the event and timing of the Rapture into the Great Tribulation. The exact timing of the Rapture cannot be predicted. However, if we teach believers to recognize the signs of the times, we will be able to acknowledge and look forward to our redemption as it draws near.

Look back again at what God reveals in 1 Corinthians 15. God explains a mystery to his prophet Paul. The mystery is the rapture event. God says that not all of the saints will die, but all of us will be changed. This is both the dead in Christ and those who are still alive.

> For the Lord himself shall descend from heaven with a shout, with the voice of the archangel, and with the *trump of God:* and the dead in Christ shall rise first: then we which are alive and remain shall be caught up together with them in the clouds, to meet the Lord in the air. (1 Thess. 4:16–17, emphasis mine)

The trumpet and the Rapture are linked. First Corinthians 15 reveals the "mystery" of the Rapture and the return of Christ. Revelation 10:7 describes the seventh and last trumpet and declares that in the days of the seventh angel, when the angel *begins* to sound the last trumpet, then the "mystery of God" is completed. There can be no doubt that these Scriptures describe the same event, which is the return of Jesus Christ during the Great Tribulation. There is no other logical or simple way to explain the relationship of these passages to one another without creating contradictions. The use of the word *mystery* in both Scriptures, as well as the description of the last trumpet, tie these verses together implicitly.

First Corinthians 15 clearly states that the Rapture occurs at the last trumpet. The Revelation gives the sequence of the last trumpet. So ask yourself, if 1 Corinthians 15 is not describing the last trumpet as described in the Revelation, then what is it describing? Is 1 Corinthians 15 describing the next-to-the-last trumpet? Or is 1 Corinthians 15 describing some other trumpet not mentioned elsewhere in Scripture?

To try to explain this away is to ignore the simplicity of the Scripture and create problems in doctrine. You would need to find a way to argue that 1 Corinthians 15 is mistaken in calling the Rapture the "last trumpet." Somehow, without any supporting Scripture, you would be forced to assume that the prophet Paul did not really mean the actual last trumpet. You would be required to twist the Scripture to conform to your beliefs.

If you are considering the implications of these verses for the first time, I realize that they may be difficult to accept because of the pervasiveness of the pretribulation rapture doctrine. After I assembled all the information you are now reading, I tried to tear it apart based on my former pretribulation rapture viewpoint. But I could not escape the link between these Scriptures. Therefore, I would ask you to take a plain, open-minded, and unencumbered view of the Scripture in order to draw the logical conclusion of what God wants us to understand.

The Trumpet Begins to Sound

The Rapture occurs in the days of the seventh angel when the seventh trumpet "begins to sound." The seventh trumpet begins with the Rapture and concludes with the seventh judgment, which is recorded in Revelation 11:15: "And the seventh angel sounded; and there were great voices in heaven, saying, The kingdoms of this world are become the kingdoms of our Lord, and of his Christ; and he shall reign for ever and ever."

With the Rapture, Jesus claims the earth for himself. Jesus has returned for his saints. Right after the Rapture, the sights in heaven are revealed. Notice that Revelation 11:18 records a time of reward in heaven for the servants of God. Again, the timing of the reward makes complete sense if all believers, dead and alive, have just been raptured into heaven at the beginning sound of the last trumpet.

> And the four and twenty elders, which sat before God on their seats, fell upon their faces, and worshipped God, saying, We give thee thanks, O Lord God Almighty, which art, and wast, and art to come; because thou hast taken to thee thy great power, and hast reigned. And the nations were angry, and thy wrath is come, and the time of the dead, that they should be judged, *and that thou shouldest give reward unto thy servants the prophets, and to the saints, and them that fear thy name, small and great;* and shouldest destroy them which destroy the earth. And the temple of God was opened in heaven, and there was seen in his temple the ark of his testament: and there were lightnings, and voices, and thunderings, and an earthquake, and great hail.(Rev. 11:16–19, emphasis mine)

What I find especially interesting is that the next chapter, Revelation 12, describes a war in heaven where Satan is cast out. Here is the text:

> And there was war in heaven: Michael and his angels fought against the dragon; and the dragon fought and his angels, and prevailed not; neither was their place found any more in heaven. And the great dragon was cast out, that old serpent, called the Devil, and Satan, which deceiveth the whole world: he was cast out into the earth, and his angels were cast out with him. And I heard a loud voice saying in heaven, Now is come salvation, and strength, and the kingdom of our God, and the power of his Christ: for the accuser of our brethren is cast down, which accused them before our God day and night. And they overcame him by the blood of the Lamb, and by the word of their testimony; and they loved not their lives unto the death. Therefore rejoice, ye heavens, and ye that dwell in them. Woe to the inhabiters of the earth and of the sea! for the devil is come down unto you, having great wrath, because he knoweth that he hath but a short time. (Rev. 12:7–12)

Do you see how all these Scriptures fit nicely together? Consider the timeline presented. The church and her saints are raptured away, including the dead in Christ. The entire universal church is assembled in heaven. The next phase is our judgment and reward (Rev. 11:18). Our rapture clears the path for the wrath of God, when he will destroy the wicked on the earth.

Meanwhile, on the heels of this is a war in heaven. Michael and his angels fight against the dragon, Satan, and his angels. God prevails, and Satan is cast out into the earth. In my mind, this is like an exchange of sorts. Satan is cast out of heaven when the Rapture occurs, and the elect are brought in. No one knows if the Rapture and the ejection of Satan from heaven occur at the same time, but it seems possible. Could it be that the lightning mentioned in the skies during the Rapture is Satan falling from heaven (Luke 10:18, "And he said unto them, I beheld Satan as lightning fall from heaven")? This is pure speculation on my part, but it makes for a fun discussion!

Rapture or Second Coming?

I believe the Gospels are describing the rapture event as the return of Jesus Christ. The gospel accounts parallel the Rapture as described in other sections of Scripture. None of the Scripture references below match the second coming of Christ as described in Revelation 19, where Jesus is riding on a horse with vengeance on his mind. This is why I believe the Rapture and the Second Coming are two distinct events separated by time.

Here's how the Bible describes the Rapture:

> For as the lightning, that lighteneth out of the one part under heaven, shineth unto the other part under heaven; so shall also the Son of man be in his day. (Luke 17:24)

> Now we beseech you, brethren, by the coming of our Lord Jesus Christ, and by our gathering together unto him…(2 Thess. 2:1)

> For the Lord himself shall descend from heaven with a shout, with the voice of the archangel, and with the trump of God: and the

dead in Christ shall rise first: then we which are alive and remain shall be caught up together with them in the clouds, to meet the Lord in the air: and so shall we ever be with the Lord. Wherefore comfort one another with these words. (1 Thess. 4:16–18)

Behold, he cometh with clouds; and every eye shall see him, and they also which pierced him: and all kindreds of the earth shall wail because of him. Even so, Amen. (Rev. 1:7)

THE RAPTURE DESCRIBED

- The entire earth will see him
- He will be in the clouds only
- Angels are sent to gather his elect from all over the earth
- There is a great sound of a trumpet
- The saints are caught up together with him in the clouds
- This is the last trump
- The mystery of God is revealed

Based on these Scriptures, we can easily document what to expect at the return of Christ during the great tribulation rapture event. The Bible teaches that the entire earth will see Jesus and that he will come in the clouds. The angels will be sent to gather his elect from over all the earth. All of this will be accompanied by the great sound of a trumpet. The saints will be caught up together with Jesus in the clouds. This is the last trumpet and reveals the mystery of God.

THE PRETRIBULATION RAPTURE IS NOT BELIEVABLE

At this point, let's circle back to the pretribulation rapture doctrine. As I began to realize on that Sunday morning in 2010, the problem with this popular doctrine is that it does not logically fit the events described in the Scriptures, nor does it logically fit the reaction of an unbelieving world.

As outlined in the first chapter, the unbelieving world does understand the concept of the Rapture and what it means to the Christian. The doctrine is pervasive in Western society even outside the church. So let's logically think about the natural human reaction to a pretribulation rapture. If the Rapture were to happen prior to the Great Tribulation, logic would lead us to believe that nearly everyone would understand what had happened—after all, they would see Jesus himself in the air, with trumpets and angels and lightning. As it is described in Scripture, this is not a secret return! The worldwide headlines would read, "Tim LaHaye's *Left Behind* Series Is True." The Internet would be filled with blogs describing the event and how it fits with Scripture. Tweets on the Rapture would abound. The disappearance of millions could not be explained away with a UFO or the Hale Bopp comet or some other sci-fi concoction. In fact, a pretribulation rapture would leave little room for the strong delusion regarding the Antichrist to deceive people anymore.

So ask yourself this: how can the events in Revelation possibly unfold, particularly in regard to the Antichrist, if the entire world recognizes that Jesus has returned in the Rapture prior to the Great Tribulation? How would men be able to turn a blind eye to the rapture event and be easily deceived by Satan into worship of the Antichrist?

Looking Up

After the beginning sound of the seventh trumpet, the Gospels describe what happens on the earth:

> Then shall two be in the field; the one shall be taken, and the other left. Two women shall be grinding at the mill; the one shall be taken, and the other left. (Matt. 24:40–41)

> I tell you, in that night there shall be two men in one bed; the one shall be taken, and the other shall be left. Two women shall be grinding together; the one shall be taken, and the other left. Two men shall be in the field; the one shall be taken, and the other left. And they answered and said unto him, Where, Lord? And he said unto them, Wheresoever the body is, thither will the eagles be gathered together. (Luke 17:34–37)

I believe these verses describe what is happening in Israel. Believer and Jew will be side by side, driven together by persecution. But the Christian is taken and the Jew is left. What happens next fulfills the prophecy of Zechariah 12, which is also mentioned in Matthew 24:30. The Jews will see Jesus, and they will mourn for him:

> And I will pour upon the house of David, and upon the inhabitants of Jerusalem, the spirit of grace and of supplications: and they shall look upon me whom they have pierced, and they shall mourn for him, as one mourneth for his only son, and shall be in bitterness for him, as one that is in bitterness for his firstborn. In that day shall there be a great mourning in Jerusalem, as the mourning of Hadadrimmon in the valley of Megiddon. (Zech. 12:10–11)

> And then shall appear the sign of the Son of man in heaven: and then shall all the tribes of the earth mourn, and they shall see the Son of man coming in the clouds of heaven with power and great glory. (Matt. 24:30)

Zechariah is important to understand. Once the Rapture occurs, God will turn his attention to the Jews on the earth. This is an entirely different discussion of God's protection and love for the Jewish people. God will deal kindly with the Jews, as described by the minor prophets of the Old Testament and the remainder of the Revelation, before Jesus physically returns to earth at the Second Coming to set up the millennial kingdom (his one-thousand-year reign). After the Rapture, salvation is no longer offered to the Gentiles. The day of grace and mercy has passed. The Rapture is that defining moment. The believers are in heaven preparing for the marriage supper of the Lamb, and the door has been shut.

Zechariah 12:10–11, then, describes the response of Israel to the return of Christ. When the Rapture happens, the Jews finally get it. They understand that they have missed the one true Messiah, Jesus. When they see Jesus return in the clouds, they will look on him whom they have pierced, and they will mourn. They will mourn like one mourns for an only son. They will be in bitterness. The Jewish nation will finally comprehend, and this comprehension leads to bitter mourning.

However, God is not finished with the Jews. They are God's chosen people. He has a special plan for the Jews that is revealed throughout Scripture. Romans 11 uses an example of grafting wild branches into the main root of an olive tree. Historically, the Jews didn't believe, so God cut them off and grafted in the Gentiles. But Romans 11:23 says of the Jews, "And they also, if they abide not still in unbelief, shall be grafted in: for God is able to graft them in again." God is able to bring back the Jews into a belief and worship of Jesus Christ. He does this by presenting himself at the Rapture.

At this point, however, the unbelieving Gentile world has been separated by their mark, their worship of the Antichrist, and their confusion of face. Their future of everlasting punishment is secured. Nothing, not even the Rapture, will move them from their stubborn rejection of God. The stage has been set for the wrath of an Almighty God and the seven vial judgments.

BACK TO THE BEGINNING

As you read the gospel accounts, I'd ask that you remember the original question. The disciples asked for the signs of Jesus' return. In response, Jesus provided a detailed and chronological list of events. Jesus even went so far as to say, "Behold, I have foretold you *all* things" (Mark 13:23). Jesus explained the Rapture in detail. Notice that once Jesus provided the sign of the Rapture, he was done providing signs. All of the signs leading up to the return of Christ had been explained, and the disciples' question had been answered. At that point, Jesus did not elaborate on what was to happen next. There was nothing else to explain to the disciples, the church, or his saints. We are all gone. We have been raptured away.

Jesus does not elaborate on what happens after the Rapture until he reveals his Revelation to John. In Revelation, Jesus explains the rest of the prophecy. The book of Revelation is not in chronological order *in its entirety;* however, it should be noted that after the seventh trumpet in Revelation, with the exception of Revelation 13 describing the Antichrist and Revelation

18 detailing the destruction of Babylon, there is no more mention of the church, the saints, martyrs, the 144,000, or the elect.

There is simply no way to look at the entire context of Scripture and maintain the pretribulation rapture doctrine. The false expectation of a pretribulation rapture creates inconsistencies in reading Scripture that cannot be explained or justified. Jesus answered the disciples' question very plainly. Ask yourself this question again: why would Jesus go to great lengths in answering the disciples' questions about the signs of his coming if there were to be no signs? If the Rapture was to happen prior to the Great Tribulation, then it seems that all this Scripture is written in vain.

The Scripture warns us repeatedly not to be deceived by any man regarding the return of Christ. "Any man" includes me, your theology professor, your pastor, your youth group leader, your concordance author, and the "experts." We must believe that the Bible is the Word of God and take the entire view of Scripture into account. "Study to shew thyself approved so that you can rightly divide the word of truth," as 2 Timothy 2:15 urges. We must make sure we are not teaching doctrines of men, but rather the truth of the Holy Bible.

Chapter 11

THE FINAL WARNINGS OF JESUS

After Jesus explains the Rapture, he provides a very strong warning to the church as he commands us to watch for his return. We are not to become complacent, and we are not to waver in our faith. The Bible teaches that Jesus' return will not take us by surprise. We can know it is near:

> And when these things begin to come to pass, then look up, and lift up your heads; for your redemption draweth nigh. (Luke 21:28)

> But ye, brethren, are not in darkness, that that day should overtake you as a thief. (1 Thess. 5:4)

If you've made it this far, then I suspect you've harbored a lingering objection in your mind regarding the surprise aspect of the Rapture. The pretribulation rapture doctrine hammers home the concept of Jesus coming like a "thief in the night" (1 Thess. 5:2: "For yourselves know perfectly that the day of the Lord so cometh as a thief in the night") and that "no man knows the hour or the day" of his return—and after all, that emphasis is contained in Scripture itself. It's logical to conclude that the Rapture will happen secretly. Yet, is that fair to the whole context of Scripture? Look at how Jesus describes this event to his disciples:

Matthew 24:36–39

> *But of that day and hour knoweth no man, no, not the angels of heaven, but my Father only. But as the days of Noah were, so shall also the coming of the Son of man be. For as in the days that were before the flood they were eating and drinking, marrying and giving in marriage, until the day that Noe entered into the ark,*

And knew not until the flood came, and took them all away; so shall also the coming of the Son of man be.
Watch therefore: for ye know not what hour your Lord doth come.

Mark 13:32–33

But of that day and that hour knoweth no man, no, not the angels which are in heaven, neither the Son, but the Father.
Take ye heed, watch and pray: for ye know not when the time is.

These verses are indeed Scripture. However, you cannot take them out of context and present them as the only truth without considering the rest of what God has written on the subject. For example, Jesus also said the following:

So likewise ye, when ye shall see all these things, know that *it is near, even at the doors.* (Matt. 24:33, emphasis mine)

The same author who says Christ's return will be like a thief in the night also states that when we see the end-of-the-world events unfolding as detailed in the Gospels and the Revelation, then we will know that his return is near, even at the doors. Is this a contradiction? Is Jesus using doublespeak? Let's look deeper into the Word of God.

The Bible clearly states that Jesus will return like a thief in the night. But there is a qualifier to this statement found later in Scripture. The qualifier is that Jesus will return like a thief in the night *only upon those who do not know to look for his return.* The Bible states that those who live in darkness will be surprised. The key to this is found in the entire text of 1 Thessalonians 5:1–11. To make this review simple, I have inserted my commentary along with the Scripture text. We will start with the last few verses in 1 Thessalonians 4 in order to set the stage for the discussion of the Rapture in context:

For this we say unto you by the word of the Lord, that we which are alive and remain unto the coming of the Lord shall not prevent them which are asleep. For the Lord himself shall descend from heaven with a shout, with the voice of the archangel, and with the trump of God: and the dead in Christ shall rise first: then we which are alive and remain shall be caught up together with them in the clouds, to meet the Lord in the air: and so shall we ever be with the Lord. Wherefore comfort one another with these words. (1 Thess. 4:15–18)

But of the times and the seasons, brethren, ye have no need that I write unto you. For yourselves know perfectly that the day of the Lord so cometh as a thief in the night. (1 Thess. 5:1–2)

God starts this section of Scripture by seeming to close the topic on the return of Christ at the Rapture, stating that there isn't much left to explain to the church in Thessalonica about the end of times. He tells us that the church already knows about the times and the seasons, and that we know that Jesus will come as a thief in the night. Unfortunately, many Christians know this Scripture but little else. Their doctrinal knowledge ends here. They do not consider the next set of verses that further clarifies this statement and provides the qualifier to the "thief in the night" statement:

For when they shall say, Peace and safety; then sudden destruction cometh upon them, as travail upon a woman with child; and they shall not escape. *But ye, brethren, are not in darkness, that that day should overtake you as a thief.* (1 Thess. 5:3–4, emphasis mine)

This is the key qualifier. Look at the wording in verse 4. The children of God are not in darkness, and the Lord's return will not overtake us as a thief! Think about it. If you are paying attention to the signs that Jesus Christ has provided in the Gospels and in his Revelation, his return will not be a surprise. You will know the day is rapidly approaching.

This qualifier validates Jesus' words in Matthew 24:33: "So likewise ye, when ye shall see all these things, know that it is near, even at the doors." Jesus states that once we see the list of chronological events come to pass, then we will know that his return is near. Verse 4 is very plain and simple. As Christians, we are not in darkness, but rather called to light and life through Jesus Christ. If we are properly taught the sequence of events leading up to his return, then the Rapture will not overtake us as a thief in the night. The passage continues:

> Ye are all the children of light, and the children of the day: we are not of the night, nor of darkness. Therefore let us not sleep, as do others; but let us watch and be sober. (1 Thess. 5:5–6)

Look at what God requires. We are the children of light. The command to watch and be sober, found here in 1 Thessalonians, is also how Jesus starts and ends his description of the end of times in the Gospels. We must watch. We must be sober. Why? So that the day of his return will not overtake us as a thief in the night. The unbelieving world will be surprised because they live in darkness. Jesus said in Luke 21:34, "And take heed to yourselves, lest at any time your hearts be overcharged with surfeiting, and drunkenness, and cares of this life, and so that day come upon you unawares."

Jesus also explains the same concept in Revelation 3:3 when he says, "Remember therefore how thou hast received and heard, and hold fast, and repent. If therefore thou shalt not watch, I will come on thee as a thief, and thou shalt not know what hour I will come upon thee."

Notice that *if* we do not watch, *then* Jesus will come upon us as a thief, and we will not know the hour that he returns.

We must understand that the Bible is a two-edged sword, as explained in Hebrews 4:12: "For the word of God is quick, and powerful, and sharper than any twoedged sword, piercing even to the dividing asunder of soul and spirit, and of the joints and marrow, and is a discerner of the thoughts and intents of the heart." Those who live in the light will not be overtaken by the return of Christ, but those who live in darkness will be overtaken as by a thief in the night. The Bible does not contradict itself. God is explaining both sides of the two-edged sword. What side of the divider you are on will determine your level of surprise. Let's move on to the remainder of the passage:

For they that sleep sleep in the night; and they that be drunken are drunken in the night. But let us, who are of the day, be sober, putting on the breastplate of faith and love; and for an helmet, the hope of salvation. For God hath not appointed us to wrath, but to obtain salvation by our Lord Jesus Christ…(1 Thess. 5:7–9)

Verse 9 includes another objection that is often be raised against any teaching contrary to the pretribulation rapture doctrine. Some use this verse to claim that Christians will not see any of the Great Tribulation because we are "not appointed to wrath." However, this claim makes a grand assumption that the entire Great Tribulation should be considered the wrath of God. The Scripture never once identifies the entire Great Tribulation as the wrath of God. Rather, as we have earlier seen, many of the early events of the Great Tribulation will be the direct result of man's sin and warmongering, or of effects of the curse on the natural world. In the Revelation, the wrath of God is confined to the last seven judgments, the seven vials. The church will be raptured away before God pours out his wrath upon the earth in the form of the seven vial judgments. Therefore, this Scripture does not provide any proof that the church will be raptured away prior to the start of the Great Tribulation.

> …who died for us, that, whether we wake or sleep, we should live together with him. Wherefore comfort yourselves together, and edify one another, even as also ye do. (1 Thess. 5:10–11)

Finally, take note of verse 11. In relation to many of the Scriptures regarding the end times, God asks us to comfort ourselves together, to edify one another. This is a common theme. The reason God reinforces this command is because the end he describes will be a very trying time for the believer. Christians will be slaughtered. The church as we know it will disintegrate. Brothers, sisters, friends, and family will turn on us. The government will be against us. Spiritual deception will abound. During this time, we will need comfort and edification. The end of times will be very tough for the children of light, the true believers in Christ. We will desperately need one another.

No Man Knows the Hour or the Day

The next lingering objection you might have is the biblical statement that "no man knows the hour or the day" of Christ's return (Matt. 24:36). But knowing *the actual hour and day* and knowing the *nearness* of the Rapture are two separate things. Nearness and exactness are not the same. As Christians, we can know the nearness of Jesus' return if we are taught to look for the events leading up to the Rapture, but we can never know the exact timing. The Scripture provides two examples to illustrate the point. The first is Noah, and the second is Lot.

First, ask yourself these two questions. Was Noah surprised by the flood? Was Lot surprised by the destruction of Sodom and Gomorrah? The answers are *no* and *no*.

Luke 17 records that Jesus used both Noah and Lot in his example of the days leading up to his return:

> And as it was in the days of Noe, so shall it be also in the days of the Son of man. They did eat, they drank, they married wives, they were given in marriage, until the day that Noah entered into the ark, and the flood came, and destroyed them all. Likewise also as it was in the days of Lot; they did eat, they drank, they bought, they sold, they planted, they builded; but the same day that Lot went out of Sodom it rained fire and brimstone from heaven, and destroyed them all. Even thus shall it be in the day when the Son of man is revealed. (Luke 17:26–30)

Let's consider Noah's circumstances first. Noah lived in an evil generation, but he knew that the flood God had promised was near. The nearness of the flood was apparent because the work that God had required in building the ark was complete, the animals were gathered together, and God told Noah to enter the ark. Noah did not know the exact start date of the flood, but as he completed the ark, he knew that the time was quickly approaching. Noah was not in darkness, and the flood did not overtake him as a thief in the night. Noah was a child of the light and a child of the day and understood the approaching judgment. But judgment did not come until Noah was safe.

And the LORD said unto Noah, Come thou and all thy house into the ark; for thee have I seen righteous before me in this generation. (Gen. 7:1)

For yet seven days, and I will cause it to rain upon the earth forty days and forty nights; and every living substance that I have made will I destroy from off the face of the earth. (Gen. 7:4)

And it came to pass after seven days, that the waters of the flood were upon the earth. (Gen. 7:10)

God told Noah to enter the ark and then declared it would rain in seven days. Noah simply watched and waited from that point forward.

Now let's consider Lot. Lot knew that the destruction of Sodom and Gomorrah was near because the angels came to warn him:

And the men said unto Lot, Hast thou here any besides? son in law, and thy sons, and thy daughters, and whatsoever thou hast in the city, bring them out of this place: for we will destroy this place, because the cry of them is waxen great before the face of the LORD; and the LORD hath sent us to destroy it. (Gen. 19:12–13)

Lot was specifically warned, and in turn, he warned his daughters and sons-in-law of the coming destruction. Yet they would not listen or believe because they walked in darkness.

And Lot went out, and spake unto his sons in law, which married his daughters, and said, Up, get you out of this place; for the LORD will destroy this city. But he seemed as one that mocked unto his sons in law. (Gen. 19:14)

As Lot lingered in the city, the angels provided further indication that the destruction was "even at the doors" by physically removing him and his immediate family from the city.

And when the morning arose, then the angels hastened Lot, saying, Arise, take thy wife, and thy two daughters, which are here; lest thou be consumed in the iniquity of the city. And while he lingered, the men laid hold upon his hand, and upon the hand of his wife, and upon the hand of his two daughters; the LORD being merciful unto him: and they brought him forth, and set him without the city. And it came to pass, when they had brought them forth abroad, that he said, Escape for thy life; look not behind thee, neither stay thou in all the plain; escape to the mountain, lest thou be consumed. (Gen. 19:15–17)

Lot was removed before the destruction, just like the believers will be raptured before the mass destruction brought by the wrath of God.

When you line these examples up with what we reviewed in 1 Thessalonians 5, you can see that contrary to popular thought, God does not intend for the Rapture to be a complete surprise to the church. If we are the children of light and heed the Scriptures, we will know the nearness of the Rapture (though we will not know the hour or the day). We should be sober and watch for the nearness of the return of Christ so that we will not be surprised. And in fact, that is precisely what Jesus tells us to do.

The pretribulation rapture doctrine relies heavily upon the surprise element of the Rapture and our inability to predict the hour and the day. However, we must remember that *all* Scripture is profitable for doctrine, so we must not build doctrines on a few verses when other verses clearly teach something different. Those who claim today that Jesus could return at any moment and that all prophecy leading up to the return of Christ has already been fulfilled are misleading the church. I have heard exclaimed from a number of pulpits that the next prophetic event is the Rapture and that Jesus could come back this very day, possibly even before the end of the church service. This is patently false. Jesus' return is not imminent (as of this writing) because the signs of his return have not yet been fulfilled. By my count, we have only fulfilled the first two signs (multiple claims of messiahship and multiple wars and rumors of wars). That is not necessarily to say that we are not living in the last days—the other signs do not require a long time to be fulfilled. But it is to say that Jesus' return will not come upon us today.

There is another parallel between Noah, Lot, and the Rapture that is often overlooked. Noah was saved from the flood. Lot was saved from Sodom and Gomorrah. Everyone else died. The same parallel can be drawn with the Rapture. When Jesus returns, he separates the saints from the rest of the inhabitants of the earth. Apart from God's dealing with the Jews, the eternal destination of everyone else is sealed. Once the flood started, everyone died. Once the fire and brimstone started, everyone died. They did not have a second chance. The same is true of those who will be left behind at the Rapture. Unlike the scenario in *Left Behind* and other popular books and movies, which depict the struggles of new believers who are saved after the Rapture, once the Rapture occurs, the earth will no longer have any of the church in its midst. The pathway to the wrath of God is now complete, and the wrath of God will be poured out without mixture upon the earth.

Watch and Pray

Jesus finished his discourse on the end times by telling his people to watch and pray. We are not to be weary. This is a common theme in Scripture; in fact, Jesus told his disciples the same thing in the garden before the crucifixion:

> And he cometh unto the disciples, and findeth them asleep, and saith unto Peter, What, could ye not watch with me one hour? Watch and pray, that ye enter not into temptation: the spirit indeed is willing, but the flesh is weak. (Matt. 26:40–41)

This can serve as an example to us today. Just as the disciples were physically tired, we cannot allow ourselves to become spiritually tired as we await the end. It is easy to read the stories in the Old Testament and gloss over the people caught in dire situations. Since we are reading it (and not living it), we can jump to the end and see how it all worked out. For example, have you ever stopped to consider the exodus of the Jews from Egypt? They were promised the land of Israel. But they would have to fight for it first. As they journeyed, they were approaching a war campaign to eliminate the current inhabitants. Every step they took toward the Promised Land was one step closer to war (it would be a little hard to get excited about that!). Eventually they would inherit the Promised Land, but they had to traverse the battlefields first. Mentally, they didn't know how it would all work out or when it would all be done, but they had to press on in order to obtain the promise.

The problem with real life is that we have to take it moment by moment. During the difficult times, even when we know that they will eventually pass, we do not know how long we will need to endure before the outlook brightens. The sheer monotony of hard times can wear us down! Jesus' command to us anticipates this reality: when the end times get bad, even if we maintain our faith that deliverance is coming, we won't know how long we'll need to wait.

When I was a boy, I spent a few long stints in the hospital with pneumonia. I remember the long nights when I was all alone. Nothing felt good. Nothing was pleasurable. Toys and food and fun were all distant memories. All I had was the passing of time and the need to endure the sickness. I knew that I would eventually feel better, but I didn't know when. My only option was to suffer through the best I could and look forward to better days. I comforted myself in looking back at the times that had passed, knowing that I was one moment closer to getting better. It will be like this during the end times. Christians will be worn out by the Antichrist, but we must press on. During the dark night of the tribulation, we must press on. Our hope rests in the promise of his coming. He will return for us. We won't know exactly when, but we can comfort ourselves in the fact that he *will* return. Every moment that we continue to cling to our faith is a step closer to our redemption.

The Goodman and the Porter

> But know this, that if the goodman of the house had known in what watch the thief would come, he would have watched, and would not have suffered his house to be broken up. Therefore be ye also ready: for in such an hour as ye think not the Son of man

cometh. Who then is a faithful and wise servant, whom his lord hath made ruler over his household, to give them meat in due season? Blessed is that servant, whom his lord when he cometh shall find so doing. Verily I say unto you, That he shall make him ruler over all his goods. But and if that evil servant shall say in his heart, My lord delayeth his coming; and shall begin to smite his fellowservants, and to eat and drink with the drunken; the lord of that servant shall come in a day when he looketh not for him, and in an hour that he is not aware of, and shall cut him asunder, and appoint him his portion with the hypocrites: there shall be weeping and gnashing of teeth. (Matt. 24:43–51)

Jesus, the great storyteller, has given us some of the best pictures of our need to watch for his return. If the goodman of the house had known when the thief would come, he would have watched. Jesus tells us to be ready. If we think we have the hour figured out ("the hour" implies *exactness,* not nearness), Jesus again tells us that it will be different from what we speculate because we cannot predict the hour. But knowing that he *is* coming back, if we watch for him and continue in the faith, we will be considered blessed servants. However, if we fall away from the faith, lose sight of his return, and fall into wickedness, we'll have our portion with the hypocrites.

Once again, this begs the question: how can you look for a surprise rapture that could happen at any moment, today or tomorrow or the next day? The answer is that you cannot watch for the unknown. You can only watch for the known. And here, Jesus has helped us greatly by providing a sequence of signs.

The gospel of Mark records a similar parable to again illustrate the point:

For the Son of Man is as a man taking a far journey, who left his house, and gave authority to his servants, and to every man his work, and commanded the porter to watch. Watch ye therefore: for ye know not when the master of the house cometh, at even, or at midnight, or at the cockcrowing, or in the morning: lest coming suddenly he find you sleeping. And what I say unto you I say unto all, Watch. (Mark 13:34–37)

In this allegory, we are the servants in the "house" with work to do, and we all have our assigned duties (the work of the body of Christ, 1 Corinthians 12–14). The porter is commanded to watch for Christ's return. We do not know exactly when he will return, but we are to watch for the events leading up to the day.

Notice that Jesus mentions "sleeping" in this parable, which ties back into the story of the disciples sleeping in the garden of Gethsemane. In the garden, the disciples did not watch and pray, but slept. If the disciples had been paying attention to the signs that Jesus was giving them regarding his imminent crucifixion, they would not have been sleeping. Rather, they would have been on high alert. Instead, they missed all the signs and were completely surprised when Judas arrived with the arresting party. They were so surprised that they all ran away (Matt. 26:56)! They were not prepared. They were not watching. So the command is put forth by Jesus for the end-time believer: Watch. Don't get caught sleeping. Look for the signs.

I often wonder: how many Christians have been lulled to sleep by the pretribulation rapture doctrine? If we are not taught to look for the signs of his return, then we will not watch. We are highly likely to fall asleep. Much like the disciples at the crucifixion, we will not understand that time is winding down and that it is time to look up because our redemption draws near. I'm afraid that without a debate on the pretribulation rapture doctrine, the end times will come upon a large portion of the church completely unaware. We will be asleep, and when the Antichrist arrives with his arresting party, we will run away totally unprepared.

In Luke, Jesus commands us to watch and pray always. We are to pray that we will be accounted worthy to escape all these things that shall come to pass and to stand before the Son of Man. We are to pray for escape from the turmoil, the persecution, and the Antichrist when he proclaims himself as God. We are to pray that we are worthy to escape—in other words, to survive until Christ returns for us at the Rapture. Jesus says that being alive for his return is a reward for all who are worthy:

Watch ye therefore, and pray always, that ye may be accounted worthy to escape all these things that shall come to pass, and to stand before the Son of man. (Luke 21:36)

If we heed Scripture, then I recommend that we begin working this plea into our prayers. It would be quite an honor to survive to see the day of Christ's return—to be able to stand up, see the skies light up, and hear the sound of the trumpet as it proclaims the start of something completely new.

Luke records that a man named Simeon, who had the Holy Ghost upon him, was kept alive to see Jesus in his first advent:

And, behold, there was a man in Jerusalem, whose name was Simeon; and the same man was just and devout, waiting for the consolation of Israel: and the Holy Ghost was upon him. And it was revealed unto him by the Holy Ghost, that he should not see death, before he had seen the Lord's Christ. And he came by the Spirit into the temple: and when the parents brought in the child Jesus, to do for him after the custom of the law, then took he him up in his arms, and blessed God, and said, Lord, now lettest thou thy servant depart in peace, according to thy word: for mine eyes have seen thy salvation. (Luke 2:25–30)

The Bible doesn't record whether Simeon was praying for this, but it was nevertheless granted to him as an honor because he was just and devout. If we can maintain our faith and be accounted worthy, the rapture day will be one amazing day! None of the saints will be ashamed. We will have endured and stood firm in the faith of Jesus until the end. We will welcome his return.

"Nevertheless when the Son of man cometh, shall he find faith on the earth?" Luke 18:8b

Chapter 12

THE WRATH OF GOD

It is at this point in the end-times chronology that things get nasty. With the church raptured and out of the way, God begins to pour out his wrath upon the earth.

Before we go into the Scriptures on this topic, I'd like to compare the Great Tribulation and the wrath of God. If you have studied the pretribulation rapture doctrine, then you know that the doctrine claims that the church must be raptured out before the Great Tribulation because the Bible promises that we, as Christians, are saved from wrath through the blood of Jesus Christ. The basis for this teaching is the following two verses:

> And to wait for his Son from heaven, whom he raised from the dead, even Jesus, which delivered us from the wrath to come. (1 Thess. 1:10)

> Much more then, being now justified by his blood, we shall be saved from wrath through him. (Rom. 5:9)

The problem with this is that we are confusing terms. Nowhere in Scripture is the Great Tribulation defined as the wrath of God. Rather, the seven vial judgments that come toward the end of the Great Tribulation are identified as the wrath of God. To apply the wrath of God *to the entire tribulation period* is inaccurate.

A look at the original language is helpful here. The word "wrath" used in both 1 Thessalonians 1:10 and Romans 5:9 is #3709 in *Strong's Concordance* and is described as "1) anger, the natural disposition, temper, character 2) movement or agitation of the soul, impulse, desire, any violent emotion, but esp. anger 3) anger, wrath, indignation 4) anger exhibited in punishment, hence used for punishment itself a) of punishments inflicted by magistrates."

The same word is translated in Revelation 14:10 as "indignation":

> The same shall drink of the wine of the wrath of God, which is poured out without mixture into the cup of his *indignation;* and he shall be tormented with fire and brimstone in the presence of the holy angels, and in the presence of the Lamb. (Rev. 14:10, emphasis mine)

If you tie these Scriptures together, it is very easy to see that the phrase "wrath of God" used earlier in the New Testament applies directly to the seven vial judgments of Revelation. The Scripture teaches that believers are raptured at the last trumpet (the seventh trumpet) and thereby avoid the wrath of God. The saints are indeed saved from the wrath of God through the blood of Jesus, fulfilling 1 Thessalonians 1:10 and Romans 5:9. The Great Tribulation is never described as the wrath of God anywhere in Scripture. Only the seven vial judgments deserve that label.

Pretribulation Rapture Problem

Now, let's examine the sequence of events associated with the pretribulation rapture and explain how this doctrine again creates a conflict using these same Scriptures. Let's assume that Jesus returns for his church at the beginning of the tribulation, as is commonly taught. After the Rapture, multitudes from all nations are saved, as described in Revelation 7. (This is the idea behind the plot of most end-times novels.)

> After this I beheld, and, lo, a great multitude, which no man could number, of all nations, and kindreds, and people, and tongues, stood before the throne, and before the Lamb, clothed with white robes, and palms in their hands; and one of the elders answered, saying unto me, What are these which are arrayed in white robes? and whence came they? And I said unto him, Sir, thou knowest. And he said to me, These are they which came out of *great tribu-*

lation, and have washed their robes, and made them white in the blood of the Lamb. (Rev. 7:9–14, emphasis mine)

Since the Bible is very clear that a great multitude of believers comes out of the Great Tribulation, then we must admit that these believers are also counted as saints who are "justified by his blood" (Romans 5:9). Yet, according to Scripture, those who are justified by the blood of Jesus are saved from the wrath of God.

According to the pretribulation rapture doctrine, Jesus has *already returned prior to these believers coming to know Christ.* If Jesus has already returned in the pretribulation rapture, then these "tribulation saints" are alive on the earth and will experience the wrath of God as the seven vial judgments are poured out.

This creates an obvious conflict. Unless Jesus returns at a second rapture before the seven vial judgments are poured out, then 1 Thessalonians 1:10 and Romans 5:9 are not true or do not universally apply to all believers. You see, the idea of a pretribulation rapture creates a contraction in the Bible that does not exist. The Bible is not wrong. The problem is that the pretribulation rapture doctrine places the timing of the Rapture at the wrong point in the timeline and thus voids the promise of these Scriptures for multitudes of believers.

The Outpouring of Wrath

The best way to explain what the wrath of God entails is to read the Scripture directly:

And I saw another sign in heaven, great and marvellous, seven angels having the seven last plagues; for in them is filled up *the wrath of God.* And I saw as it were a sea of glass mingled with fire: and them that had gotten the victory over the beast, and over his image, and over his mark, and over the number of his name, stand on the sea of glass, having the harps of God. And they sing the song of Moses the servant of God, and the song of the Lamb, saying, Great and marvellous are thy works, Lord God Almighty; just and true are thy ways, thou King of saints. Who shall not fear thee, O Lord, and glorify thy name? for thou only art holy: for all nations shall come and worship before thee; for thy judgments are made manifest.

And after that I looked, and, behold, the temple of the tabernacle of the testimony in heaven was opened: and the seven angels came out of the temple, having the seven plagues, clothed in pure and white linen, and having their breasts girded with golden girdles. And one of the four beasts gave unto the seven angels seven golden vials full of the wrath of God, who liveth for ever and ever. And the temple was filled with smoke from the glory of God, and from his power; and no man was able to enter into the temple, till the seven plagues of the seven angels were fulfilled. (Rev. 15:1–8, emphasis mine)

Revelation 15:8 says that during this time in heaven, the temple in heaven will be off-limits to every man because God is pouring out his wrath on the earth. There will not be anyone "justified by the blood of Christ" on the earth during this time. God will protect the Jews, but the Jews left on the earth will not have been redeemed by Christ. God will deal with them in a different fashion.

The wrath of God described in Revelation makes the previous judgments look mild by comparison. This truly is the wrath of God without question. Revelation 16 describes the horrors that await:

And I heard a great voice out of the temple saying to the seven angels, Go your ways, and pour out the vials of the wrath of God upon the earth.

And the first went, and poured out his vial upon the earth; and there fell a noisome and grievous sore upon the men which had the mark of the beast, and upon them which worshipped his image.

And the second angel poured out his vial upon the sea; and it became as the blood of a dead man: and every living soul died in the sea.

Rapture: Delayed?

And the third angel poured out his vial upon the rivers and fountains of waters; and they became blood. And I heard the angel of the waters say, Thou art righteous, O Lord, which art, and wast, and shalt be, because thou hast judged thus. For they have shed the blood of saints and prophets, and thou hast given them blood to drink; for they are worthy. And I heard another out of the altar say, Even so, Lord God Almighty, true and righteous are thy judgments.

And the fourth angel poured out his vial upon the sun; and power was given unto him to scorch men with fire. And men were scorched with great heat, and blasphemed the name of God, which hath power over these plagues: and they repented not to give him glory.

And the fifth angel poured out his vial upon the seat of the beast; and his kingdom was full of darkness; and they gnawed their tongues for pain, and blasphemed the God of heaven because of their pains and their sores, and repented not of their deeds.

And the sixth angel poured out his vial upon the great river Euphrates; and the water thereof was dried up, that the way of the kings of the east might be prepared. And I saw three unclean spirits like frogs come out of the mouth of the dragon, and out of the mouth of the beast, and out of the mouth of the false prophet. For they are the spirits of devils, working miracles, which go forth unto the kings of the earth and of the whole world, to gather them to the battle of that great day of God Almighty.

Behold, I come as a thief. Blessed is he that watcheth, and keepeth his garments, lest he walk naked, and they see his shame.

And he gathered them together into a place called in the Hebrew tongue Armageddon. And the seventh angel poured out his vial into the air; and there came a great voice out of the temple of heaven, from the throne, saying, It is done. And there were voices, and thunders, and lightnings; and there was a great earthquake, such as was not since men were upon the earth, so mighty an earthquake, and so great. And the great city was divided into three parts, and the cities of the nations fell: and great Babylon came in remembrance before God, to give unto her the cup of the wine of the fierceness of his wrath. And every island fled away, and the mountains were not found. And there fell upon men a great hail out of heaven, every stone about the weight of a talent: and men blasphemed God because of the plague of the hail; for the plague thereof was exceeding great.

The Bible says we as Christians are and will be saved from the wrath of God, and for that I am thankful. These last plagues will all but destroy the earth. I can't even begin to describe how disruptive, destructive, and deadly this period of time will be.

The 2 Thessalonians Timeline

When I finally understood that the Rapture occurs at the last trumpet recorded in Revelation, then 2 Thessalonians 1:5–10 became an obvious overview of the entire timeline. This timeline includes persecution, the tribulation, the fifth seal in Revelation, and then the Rapture when Jesus will be revealed from heaven with his mighty angels. After the Rapture, the next event is the wrath of God, when Jesus will take vengeance on those who do not know God. They will be punished with everlasting destruction from the presence of the Lord. Finally, the passage references the Second Coming, when Jesus shall come to be glorified in his saints and to be admired in all them that believe. Here's how it reads:

> Which is a manifest token of the righteous judgment of God, that ye may be counted worthy of the kingdom of God, for which ye also suffer: seeing it is a righteous thing with God to recompense tribulation to them that trouble you; and to you who are troubled *rest with us,* when the Lord Jesus shall be revealed from heaven with his mighty angels, in flaming fire taking vengeance on them that know not God, and that obey not the gospel of our Lord Jesus Christ: who shall be punished with everlasting destruction from the presence of the Lord, and from the glory of his power; when

he shall come to be glorified in his saints, and to be admired in all them that believe (because our testimony among you was believed) in that day. (2 Thess. 1:5–10, emphasis mine)

The Bible is extremely consistent in its description of the end times. The only inconsistency is found when you try to force fit a pretribulation rapture event before the Great Tribulation instead of one that occurs at some point during the Great Tribulation. The simple timeline of the end is hard to miss.

I've always been impressed at how neatly the Bible fits together as a cohesive whole, from Genesis to Revelation. Even across fifteen hundred plus years and a number of different writers from various backgrounds, the message from God remains consistent. The same is true with the timeline presented in this book. God will separate his people from the rest of the world throughout the trials and tribulations of the end times, and ultimately through his divine deliverance at the Rapture. Those remaining will be forced to deal with the wrath of a righteous judge.

Chapter 13

CHILDREN OF THE GREAT TRIBULATION

In regard to the wrath of God and the Rapture, the question will always arise: "But what about the children?" We have a hard time believing that God would simply destroy unbelieving children without giving them a real chance to choose him. Some teach that all children will be raptured, but there is no basis for believing that in Scripture. So what does Scripture say about children? When I discovered Scripture's teaching on this topic, I was quite surprised that I had overlooked it for so many years and had never heard it taught. I have to confess to you: this is one of my favorite chapters in the book!

The Marriage Supper of the Lamb

As a prelude to our discussion of the children, let's turn our attention to the believers in heaven. At this point, believers have been raptured, judged, and rewarded. The next event in heaven is the marriage supper of the Lamb. This is a picture of the marriage of Jesus and his church.

We all love a wedding, right? There is always an air of excitement and anticipation as the big day arrives. Even if you are just a guest, you can still feel the buzz. If you have ever been a bride or groom, then you can identify with the heightened sense of joy and nervousness on this day of all days. The Bible says that we aren't just *guests* at the marriage supper of the Lamb; we are participants. We are the bride.

> Let us be glad and rejoice, and give honour to him: for the marriage of the Lamb is come, and his wife hath made herself ready. And to her was granted that she should be arrayed in fine linen, clean and white: for the fine linen is the righteousness of saints. And he saith unto me, Write, Blessed are they which are called unto the marriage

supper of the Lamb. And he saith unto me, These are the true sayings of God. (Rev. 19:7–9)

We will be glad and rejoice! Even though we were born into sin, we are allowed to wear white. We will have nothing to be ashamed of. We will be clothed in righteousness, as Isaiah long ago promised: "Come now, and let us reason together, saith the LORD: though your sins be as scarlet, they shall be as white as snow; though they be red like crimson, they shall be as wool" (Isa. 1:18). The blood of Jesus Christ has washed us clean. God has changed our garments, much like in the vision in Zechariah:

> And he shewed me Joshua the high priest standing before the angel of the LORD, and Satan standing at his right hand to resist him. And the LORD said unto Satan, The LORD rebuke thee, O Satan; even the LORD that hath chosen Jerusalem rebuke thee: is not this a brand plucked out of the fire? Now Joshua was clothed with filthy garments, and stood before the angel. And he answered and spake unto those that stood before him, saying, Take away the filthy garments from him. And unto him he said, Behold, I have caused thine iniquity to pass from thee, and I will clothe thee with change of raiment. And I said, Let them set a fair mitre upon his head. So they set a fair mitre upon his head, and clothed him with garments. And the angel of the LORD stood by. (Zech. 3:1–5)

After the marriage supper of the Lamb, Jesus is ready to take back his possession. Jesus is ready to return to earth. The Bible describes this return in Revelation 19 as well as Zechariah 14.

Armageddon and the Second Coming of Christ

The second coming of Christ coincides with Armageddon. This is the ultimate confrontation of good versus evil. At this point, the whole world gears up for war. The forces of earth assemble in a place called Armageddon:

And I saw three unclean spirits like frogs come out of the mouth of the dragon, and out of the mouth of the beast, and out of the mouth of the false prophet. For they are the spirits of devils, working miracles, which go forth unto the kings of the earth and of the whole world, to gather them to the battle of that great day of God Almighty. And he gathered them together into a place called in the Hebrew tongue Armageddon. (Rev. 16:13–16)

Behold, the day of the LORD cometh, and thy spoil shall be divided in the midst of thee. For I will gather all nations against Jerusalem to battle; and the city shall be taken, and the houses rifled, and the women ravished; and half of the city shall go forth into captivity, and the residue of the people shall not be cut off from the city. (Zech. 14:1–2)

After the nations are gathered together for war, the heavens open, and the Word of God, Jesus Christ, comes forth riding a white horse. His eyes are described as a "flame of fire." He is wearing many crowns. His clothes are dipped in blood. His thigh is tattooed with the words, "King of kings and Lord of lords." The kingdom of God on earth is coming, and Jesus will at last stake his claim.

Then shall the LORD go forth, and fight against those nations, as when he fought in the day of battle. (Zech. 14:3)

And I saw heaven opened, and behold a white horse; and he that sat upon him was called Faithful and True, and in righteousness he doth judge and make war. His eyes were as a flame of fire, and on his head were many crowns; and he had a name written, that no man knew, but he himself. And he was clothed with a vesture dipped in blood: and his name is called The Word of God. And the armies which were in heaven followed him upon white horses, clothed in fine linen, white and clean. (Rev. 19:11–14)

Notice that in verse 14, the armies of heaven follow Christ on white horses, clothed in fine linen, white and clean. These are the same garments that were given to the saints at the marriage supper of the Lamb in Revelation 19:8, where the saints are described as "arrayed in fine linen, clean and white: for the fine linen is the righteousness of saints." There is no doubt that the armies of heaven consist of the saints.

This serves to further confirm the timing of the Rapture. In order for us to be in heaven for the marriage and to be part of this army, we must first be taken to heaven in the rapture. The sequence of events indicates a separation between the gathering of the saints (the Rapture) and the second coming of Christ (the return). Revelation 19 continues to describe the Second Coming:

> And out of his mouth goeth a sharp sword, that with it he should smite the nations: and he shall rule them with a rod of iron: and he treadeth the winepress of the fierceness and wrath of Almighty God. And he hath on his vesture and on his thigh a name written, KING OF KINGS, AND LORD OF LORDS. And I saw an angel standing in the sun; and he cried with a loud voice, saying to all the fowls that fly in the midst of heaven, Come and gather yourselves together unto the supper of the great God; that ye may eat the flesh of kings, and the flesh of captains, and the flesh of mighty men, and the flesh of horses, and of them that sit on them, and the flesh of all men, both free and bond, both small and great. And I saw the beast, and the kings of the earth, and their armies, gathered together to make war against him that sat on the horse, and against his army. (Rev. 19:15–19)

The Word of God physically returns to earth, and the Antichrist is prepared to do battle. But Christ prevails. He stands upon the Mount of Olives, causing an earthquake…and the lighting is all wrong.

> And his feet shall stand in that day upon the mount of Olives, which is before Jerusalem on the east, and the mount of Olives

shall cleave in the midst thereof toward the east and toward the west, and there shall be a very great valley; and half of the mountain shall remove toward the north, and half of it toward the south. And ye shall flee to the valley of the mountains; for the valley of the mountains shall reach unto Azal: yea, ye shall flee, like as ye fled from before the earthquake in the days of Uzziah king of Judah: and the LORD my God shall come, and all the saints with thee. And it shall come to pass in that day, that the light shall not be clear, nor dark: but it shall be one day which shall be known to the LORD, not day, nor night: but it shall come to pass, that at evening time it shall be light. (Zech. 14:4–7)

The victory is the Lord's, and he reclaims his property—the whole of creation. He takes the Antichrist and the false prophet and casts them, alive, into a lake of fire:

Thine, O LORD is the greatness, and the power, and the glory, and the victory, and the majesty: for all that is in the heaven and in the earth is thine; thine is the kingdom, O LORD, and thou art exalted as head above all. (1 Chron. 29:11)

And the beast was taken, and with him the false prophet that wrought miracles before him, with which he deceived them that had received the mark of the beast, and them that worshipped his image. These both were cast alive into a lake of fire burning with brimstone. And the remnant were slain with the sword of him that sat upon the horse, which sword proceeded out of his mouth: and all the fowls were filled with their flesh. (Rev. 19:20–21)

Zechariah is more descriptive of how the enemy is destroyed. The Bible describes a plague that consumes the flesh so quickly that the victims are still standing when it happens (I always think of the Nazi who melts away at the end of *Raiders of the Lost Ark*). In addition to the flesh-eating plague, God will cause the inhabitants of the earth who are not physically at Armegeddon to turn against one another and kill each other:

> And this shall be the plague wherewith the LORD will smite all the people that have fought against Jerusalem; Their flesh shall consume away while they stand upon their feet, and their eyes shall consume away in their holes, and their tongue shall consume away in their mouth. And it shall come to pass in that day, that a great tumult from the LORD shall be among them; and they shall lay hold every one on the hand of his neighbour, and his hand shall rise up against the hand of his neighbour. And Judah also shall fight at Jerusalem; and the wealth of all the heathen round about shall be gathered together, gold, and silver, and apparel, in great abundance. And so shall be the plague of the horse, of the mule, of the camel, and of the ass, and of all the beasts that shall be in these tents, as this plague. (Zech. 14:12–15)

THE KINGDOM ESTABLISHED

After the war, God establishes his kingdom upon the earth. The saints are a part of the new government. Revelation 5 and Revelation 20 describe a new song in heaven that proclaims that the Lamb has redeemed the saints from every nation by his blood. And the Lamb has made us kings and priests, and we shall reign upon the earth.

> And when he had taken the book, the four beasts and four and twenty elders fell down before the Lamb, having every one of them harps, and golden vials full of odours, which are the prayers of saints. And they sung a new song, saying, Thou art worthy to take the book, and to open the seals thereof: for thou wast slain, and hast redeemed us to God by thy blood out of every kindred, and tongue, and people, and nation; and hast made us unto our God kings and priests: and we shall reign on the earth. (Rev. 5:8–10)

> And I saw thrones, and they sat upon them, and judgment was given unto them: and I saw the souls of them that were beheaded for the witness of Jesus, and for the word of God, and which had not worshipped the beast, neither his image, neither had received his mark upon their foreheads, or in their hands; and they lived and reigned with Christ a thousand years. But the rest of the dead lived not again until the thousand years were finished. This is the first resurrection. Blessed and holy is he that hath part in the first resurrection: on such the second death hath no power, but they shall be priests of God and of Christ, and shall reign with him a thousand years. (Rev. 20:4–6)

Zechariah and Isaiah further describe the kingdom of God: God will establish a kingdom centered around Jerusalem. All nations will gather to Jerusalem on an annual basis to worship the king and to keep the feast of the tabernacle. Isaiah says that the forces of the Gentiles shall come to Jerusalem. If any nations do not obey, then God will withhold rain from their land.

This is where things get interesting. By now you may be asking, what does all this have to do with the children? Before I explain, see if you can identify the answer within these Scriptures for yourself:

> And it shall be in that day, that living waters shall go out from Jerusalem; half of them toward the former sea, and half of them toward the hinder sea: in summer and in winter shall it be. And the Lord shall be king over all the earth: in that day shall there be one Lord, and his name one. All the land shall be turned as a plain from Geba to Rimmon south of Jerusalem: and it shall be lifted up, and inhabited in her place, from Benjamin's gate unto the place of the first gate, unto the corner gate, and from the tower of Hananeel unto the king's winepresses. And men shall dwell in it, and there shall be no more utter destruction; but Jerusalem shall be safely inhabited…
>
> And it shall come to pass, that every one that is left of all the

nations which came against Jerusalem shall even go up from year to year to worship the King, the LORD of hosts, and to keep the feast of tabernacles. And it shall be, that whoso will not come up of all the families of the earth unto Jerusalem to worship the King, the LORD of hosts, even upon them shall be no rain. And if the family of Egypt go not up, and come not, that have no rain; there shall be the plague, wherewith the LORD will smite the heathen that come not up to keep the feast of tabernacles. This shall be the punishment of Egypt, and the punishment of all nations that come not up to keep the feast of tabernacles.

In that day shall there be upon the bells of the horses, HOLINESS UNTO THE LORD; and the pots in the LORD's house shall be like the bowls before the altar. Yea, every pot in Jerusalem and in Judah shall be holiness unto the LORD of hosts: and all they that sacrifice shall come and take of them, and seethe therein: and in that day there shall be no more the Canaanite in the house of the LORD of hosts. (Zech. 14:8–11, 16–21)

Arise, shine; for thy light is come, and the glory of the LORD is risen upon thee. For, behold, the darkness shall cover the earth, and gross darkness the people: but the LORD shall arise upon thee, and his glory shall be seen upon thee. And the Gentiles shall come to thy light, and kings to the brightness of thy rising. Lift up thine eyes round about, and see: all they gather themselves together, they come to thee: *thy sons* shall come from far, and *thy daughters* shall be nursed at thy side.

Then thou shalt see, and flow together, and thine heart shall fear, and be enlarged; because the abundance of the sea shall be converted unto thee, the forces of the Gentiles shall come unto thee. The multitude of camels shall cover thee, the dromedaries of Midian and Ephah; all they from Sheba shall come: they shall bring gold and incense; and they shall shew forth the praises of the LORD.

All the flocks of Kedar shall be gathered together unto thee, the rams of Nebaioth shall minister unto thee: they shall come up with acceptance on mine altar, and I will glorify the house of my glory.

Who are these that fly as a cloud, and as the doves to their windows? Surely the isles shall wait for me, and the ships of Tarshish first, to bring *thy sons* from far, their silver and their gold with them, unto the name of the LORD thy God, and to the Holy One of Israel, because he hath glorified thee. And the *sons of strangers* shall build up thy walls, and their kings shall minister unto thee: for in my wrath I smote thee, but in my favour have I had mercy on thee.

Therefore thy gates shall be open continually; they shall not be shut day nor night; that men may bring unto thee the forces of the Gentiles, and that their kings may be brought. For the nation and kingdom that will not serve thee shall perish; yea, those nations shall be utterly wasted. The glory of Lebanon shall come unto thee, the fir tree, the pine tree, and the box together, to beautify the place of my sanctuary; and I will make the place of my feet glorious. *The sons* also of them that afflicted thee shall come bending unto thee; and all they that despised thee shall bow themselves down at the soles of thy feet; and they shall call thee; The city of the LORD, The Zion of the Holy One of Israel.

Whereas thou has been forsaken and hated, so that no man went through thee, I will make thee an eternal excellency, a joy of many generations. Thou shalt also suck the milk of the Gentiles, and shalt suck the breast of kings: and thou shalt know that I the LORD am thy Saviour and thy Redeemer, the mighty one of Jacob. For brass I will bring gold, and for iron I will bring silver, and for wood brass, and for stones iron: I will also make thy officers peace, and thine exactors righteousness. Violence shall no more be heard in thy land, wasting nor destruction within thy borders; but thou shalt call thy walls Salvation, and thy gates Praise. The sun shall be no more thy light by day; neither for brightness shall the moon give light unto thee: but the LORD shall be unto thee an everlasting light, and thy God thy glory. Thy sun shall no more go down; neither shall thy moon withdraw itself: for the LORD shall be thine everlasting light, and the days of thy mourning shall be ended.

Thy people also shall be all righteous: they shall inherit the land for ever, the branch of my planting, the work of my hands, that I may be glorified. *A little one* shall become a thousand, and *a small one* a strong nation: I the LORD will hasten it in his time. (Isa. 60, emphasis mine)

Where Do These People in the Millennium Come From?

Before we address the children directly, we need to consider a logical question: where do all the people of all nations come from?

If we take a minute to review the great tribulation rapture timeline, we will notice that there appears to be a population problem:

The Great Tribulation Rapture Timeline

- Great tribulation: lots of people die.
- Rapture: all the saints are removed from the earth.
- Wrath of God (vial judgments): only the Jews and those who worship the Antichrist are left on earth during this period.
- Marriage supper of the Lamb in heaven.
- The second coming of Jesus Christ.
- Armageddon: the worshipers of Antichrist are destroyed.
- The kingdom of God is established over all nations and people.

According to the timeline, all the saints are raptured away. The worshipers of Antichrist are destroyed at Armageddon, killed by the flesh-eating plague described in Zechariah 14, or killed by each other. Yet, Isaiah and Zechariah describe multitudes of people from all nations who inhabit the kingdom of God during the millennium. If all this happens as described in the Bible, then where do the people of all nations during the millennium come from?

The pretribulation rapture doctrine claims that this dilemma proves the validity of their teaching. Its proponents believe that the pretribulation rapture occurs, followed by the Great Tribulation wherein multitudes are saved. The multitudes of great tribulation saints populate the earth at the second coming of Christ. However, this creates a problem, because if this doctrine is correct, the great tribulation saints are not spared from the wrath of God, which violates Romans 5:9 and 1 Thessalonians 5:9, and they must also miss the marriage supper of the Lamb.

Children of the Millennium

The dilemma regarding the source of human population during the millennium is easily solved. The answer is children.

We are often taught that the rapture of the church will include all children (saved and unsaved). However, this is not stated anywhere in Scripture. God's plan could easily consist of one of these two options:

1. All children, both saved and unsaved, are raptured at the beginning sound of the seventh trumpet. Even if all the children of earth are gone, there is still time between the Rapture and the Second Coming for children to be born. God controls the womb (Gen. 30:22, "And God remembered Rachel, and God hearkened to her, and opened her womb"), so God can ensure there are children born before his second coming. God claims in Isaiah and elsewhere his authority to open and close the womb (Isa. 66:9, "Shall I bring to the birth, and not cause to bring forth? saith the Lord: shall I cause to bring forth, and shut the womb? saith thy God").
2. Unsaved children are not raptured. This of course will cause many people to fear that their young children will be left behind to fend for themselves, and they protest that a just God would not do this. But we must remember that if God can create a child in the womb, then he certainly has the power to protect a child outside of the womb, even if the parents are absent. Is it possible that we are willing to trust God with our eternal souls for salvation, but we don't want to trust him with our children? Think about it.

I believe that a just and holy God will treat children differently than he does adults. This is not just my preference: it is evident in Scripture. For example, look at the history of Israel after the exodus from Egypt. God became very angry with the Israelites because of their unbelief—so angry, in fact, that he decided to kill all of them and raise up a nation from Moses alone. Moses pleaded for mercy and forgiveness on behalf of the Israelites, and God granted Moses his request—but only partially. With a few exceptions, God drew a line at twenty years of age, where anyone above the age of twenty would die in the wilderness while anyone below the age of twenty would be granted access to the Promised Land.

> And the LORD said, I have pardoned according to thy word: but as truly as I live, all the earth shall be filled with the glory of the LORD. Because all those men which have seen my glory, and my miracles, which I did in Egypt and in the wilderness, and have tempted me now these ten times, and have not hearkened to my voice; surely they shall not see the land which I sware unto their fathers, neither shall any of them that provoked me see it: but my servant Caleb, because he had another spirit with him, and hath followed me fully, him will I bring into the land whereinto he went; and his seed shall possess it. (Now the Amalekites and the Canaanites dwelt in the valley.) Tomorrow turn you, and get you into the wilderness by the way of the Red sea.
>
> And the LORD spake unto Moses and unto Aaron, saying, How long shall I bear with this evil congregation, which murmur against me? I have heard the murmurings of the children of Israel, which they murmur against me. Say unto them, As truly as I live, saith the LORD, as ye have spoken in mine ears, so will I do to you: your carcases shall fall in this wilderness; and all that were numbered of you, according to your whole number, *from twenty years old and upward* which have murmured against me. Doubtless ye shall not come into the land, concerning which I sware to make you dwell therein, save Caleb the son of Jephunneh, and Joshua the son of Nun. *But your little ones,* which ye said should be a prey,

them will I bring in, and they shall know the land which ye have despised. But as for you, your carcases, they shall fall in this wilderness. And your children shall wander in the wilderness forty years, and bear your whoredoms, until your carcases be wasted in the wilderness. (Num. 14:20–33, emphasis mine)

Just like the Promised Land, populated by children twenty years and younger, God's kingdom is going to be populated by children who are on the earth at the Second Coming. Look at the words of Jesus himself concerning his kingdom:

But Jesus said, Suffer little children, and forbid them not, to come unto me: for of such is the kingdom of heaven. (Matt. 19:14)

But when Jesus saw it, he was much displeased, and said unto them, Suffer the little children to come unto me, and forbid them not: for of such is the kingdom of God. (Mark 10:14)

But Jesus called them unto him, and said, Suffer little children to come unto me, and forbid them not: for of such is the kingdom of God. (Luke 18:16)

While the Scriptures quoted here could (and almost certainly do) have other meanings as well, the real proof is found in Isaiah 60, which we reviewed earlier in this chapter. Did you notice the answer when you read it? In Isaiah, the people of the millennium are described as "sons," "daughters," "little ones," and "small ones" in no fewer than six different references.

And the Gentiles shall come to thy light, and kings to the brightness of thy rising. Lift up thine eyes round about, and see: all they gather themselves together, they come to thee: *thy sons* shall come from far, and *thy daughters* shall be nursed at thy side. (Isa. 60:3–4)

And the *sons of strangers* shall build up thy walls, and their kings shall minister unto thee: for in my wrath I smote thee, but in my favour have I had mercy on thee. (Isa. 60:10)

The sons also of them that afflicted thee shall come bending unto thee; and all they that despised thee shall bow themselves down at the soles of thy feet; and they shall call thee; The city of the LORD, The Zion of the Holy One of Israel. (Isa. 60:14)

A little one shall become a thousand, and a *small one* a strong nation: I the LORD will hasten it in his time.(Isa. 60:22)

Isaiah 60:22 is the key verse. From a little one and a small one, God will quickly raise up strong nations. However God works out the final plan, there will be many "little ones" on the earth who, due to their age, will not be subject to the same treatment as adults when Christ returns at the Second Coming. The population of the millennium will be drawn from these little ones from all nations, as specifically prophesied by Isaiah.

THE NUMBERS

At this point, you may be wondering about the scientific credibility of such a theory. According to the United Nations population statistics, in 2010 there were approximately 6.895 billion people on the earth.[20]

For the same time period, the UN estimates that 27 percent of the world's population was under the age of fifteen.[21]

At the time of this writing in 2011, this calculates to an approximate 1.865 billion children under the age of fifteen. During the Great Tribulation, there will be massive turmoil, war, famine, disease, and natural and supernatural disasters. Yet, even if the population under the age of fifteen were reduced by 99.5 percent, there would still be 9.3 million children left alive on the earth.

The worldwide average number of births in a year is currently 140 million.[22]

In a short time span, even during the worst of the Great Tribulation, there could be millions of young children born across all nations.

Regardless of what statistics might prove, we cannot escape the sovereignty of God. If God wants people on the earth, then there will be people on the earth. Period. God does whatever he pleases. When Elijah was depressed and ready to give up because he assumed that he was the only one left to follow God, God told him that he had reserved a remnant:

> But what saith the answer of God unto him? I have reserved to myself seven thousand men, who have not bowed the knee to the image of Baal. (Rom. 11:4, citing 1 Kings 19:18)

> But our God is in the heavens: he hath done whatsoever he hath pleased. (Ps. 115:3)

God reserved the remnant in Elijah's day. In the millennium, God will reserve a remnant and raise up nations from little ones. The sons of the strangers will rebuild Jerusalem. The sons of the men who afflicted and despised the Jews will come and bow down before them. God will fulfill his will.

The End of the Millennium

The kingdom of God on the earth will last for one thousand years. In the end, God will allow Satan to once again influence the world:

> And when the thousand years are expired, Satan shall be loosed out of his prison, and shall go out to deceive the nations which are in the four quarters of the earth, Gog, and Magog, to gather them together to battle: the number of whom is as the sand of the sea. And they went up on the breadth of the earth, and compassed the camp of the saints about, and the beloved city: and fire came down from God out of heaven, and devoured them. (Rev. 20:7–9)

Why would God allow Satan out to deceive these millennial people and the nations? While Scripture does not explicitly tell us, I believe that it is because we *all* must make a choice. There is not a single created being in heaven who did not choose either good or evil. The angels had to choose between God and Satan. One-third of the angels followed Satan. All humans make a choice, and we either follow God and his Son Jesus Christ or we don't. During the millennium, humans will be born, but since God is among them, they won't really have a choice until Satan is released for a season. At that point, they must choose.

Once again, there will be a short-lived battle that God easily wins. Satan will then be cast into the lake of fire:

> And the devil that deceived them was cast into the lake of fire and brimstone, where the beast and the false prophet are, and shall be tormented day and night for ever and ever. (Rev. 20:10)

The Day of Judgment

At last, the day of judgment for unbelievers now arrives. The day that all men should fear. The day when a holy and righteous king will judge the people. The believers already have been judged and rewarded as described in Revelation 11. Now is the time for the unbelievers to be judged and punished. The face of the king is described as so fearful that the earth and heavens want to flee away, but they cannot escape. No one can escape. All will bow before him.

> And I saw a great white throne, and him that sat on it, from whose face the earth and the heaven fled away; and there was found no place for them. And I saw the dead, small and great, stand before God; and the books were opened: and another book was opened, which is the book of life: and the dead were judged out of those things which were written in the books, according to their works. And the sea gave up the dead which were in it; and death and hell delivered up the dead which were in them: and they were judged every man according to their works. And death and hell were cast into the lake of fire. This is the second death. And whosoever was not found written in the book of life was cast into the lake of fire. (Rev. 20:11–15)

≽ Rapture: Delayed? ≼

Eternal separation from God and the second death await those who reject the king, Jesus Christ. If you are reading this, then it is not too late. God should truly be feared, and also loved, because he has provided a way to escape his righteous judgment. Today, the salvation of God is extended to all.

Chapter 14

THE SALVATION OF GOD: COME ONE, COME ALL

Many today speculate that we are living in the last generation. Whether this is true or not, one thing is certain: *you* are living in your last generation. You have one short life that the Bible describes as a vapor, and this life is being quickly used up moment by moment, day by day, month after month, year after year.

Each of us must decide whether to believe the God of the Bible and his Son Jesus Christ, or to ignore and reject him. Indecision is a decision. What will you do?

God should be feared: we have clearly seen that in our study of the end times as laid out in the Scriptures. But he also should be loved because of his mercy and patience toward us—and that is the main focus of the rest of the New Testament, and indeed, of all of Scripture. Romans 5:8 sums up the incredible message in these few words: "But God commendeth his love toward us, in that, while we were yet sinners, Christ died for us." God has provided a way of salvation for each of us.

God created everything around us, from the physical world to the societies we live in, including the institutions of family and government. The beauty of the Bible is that God uses the basic concepts of his creation to illustrate and teach us things about himself. For example, the Bible repeatedly uses the concept of God as a Father. Many of us understand this relationship because of our families. But if your father was not a good or present part of your life, God offers another example of his place in our lives as a king. In either case, the concept in view is our relationship to authority. The absolute ruling power of a king is well understood by many cultures, and even in the United States, the authority of a king still exists as a strong theme in popular movies and other cultural expressions (*Lord of the Rings,* anyone?). Think about this concept as it relates to you.

God the Father and the King of kings has stated his intentions very specifically in the Bible. He has told us exactly what he is going to do with each living soul and why. God is in control and has established the ground rules and requirements for salvation, ground rules that must be followed. You either accept them, partially accept them, or reject them. You believe and accept his way and it changes your life, or you believe it but it has no impact on your life, or you reject it altogether. But your response does not change the reality. That is the way authority works.

Here's a personal example: getting the children to bed in my house is an exercise of organized chaos. If you have ever heard Bill Cosby's monologue about getting his kid to bed, then you will get a picture of the nightly routine at my house. On one occasion, I gave my son a deadline to have his teeth brushed and be in bed by 8:30. I warned him that if he did not comply, he would be punished. I gave him specific instructions and told him exactly what would happen if he did not obey.

At 8:30, my son was in bed, but his teeth were not brushed. At that point, he was disciplined. As he was expressing his dismay at his predicament, I was reminded of our relationship to God the Father. My son knew exactly what his fate would be if he did not both believe and obey. However, this did not change his behavior. If you were to ask my son if he believed his father would follow through with the punishment, he would have said yes. However, the belief was not enough to impact his behavior.

God has stated his intentions and commands in the Bible. As individuals, we can do what God has commanded, or we can ignore him and be punished. The problem for many in the judgment day will be that they simply did not believe God. Others will claim belief, but the belief never turned into obedience. God has stated exactly what he intends to do, and he will fulfill his promises. You will not have any arguments or ways to justify yourself before God. There will be many who claim belief in God, but the Word of God stands in judgment:

> This people draweth nigh unto me with their mouth, and honoureth me with their lips; but their heart is far from me. (Matt. 15:8)

And why call ye me, Lord, Lord, and do not the things which I say? (Luke 6:46)

In order to gain access to God and his kingdom, you must be willing to believe in the Holy One of God, Jesus Christ, and to live your life in submission to him. This is the gospel—literally, "good news." Jesus said of himself in Luke 4:18–19, "The Spirit of the Lord is upon me, because he hath anointed me to preach the gospel to the poor; he hath sent me to heal the brokenhearted, to preach deliverance to the captives, and recovering of sight to the blind, to set at liberty them that are bruised, to preach the acceptable year of the Lord." Jesus also explained in John 3:17, "For God sent not his Son into the world to condemn the world; but that the world through him might be saved."

God desires that we all come to the knowledge of salvation through Jesus Christ. The Bible records in 2 Peter 3:9 that "The Lord is not slack concerning his promise, as some men count slackness; but is longsuffering to us-ward, not willing that any should perish, but that all should come to repentance." God is very patient. His call is a worldwide call to salvation and acceptance before him.

A Humble and Contrite Heart

God is very clear that he favors a humble and contrite person. We must come to understand our place in the world and our relationship to God. If we are willing to look beyond our current existence, then we can begin to understand how small we are compared to how great God is! Our lives, regardless of success or status, are very short and quickly forgotten:

> As he came forth of his mother's womb, naked shall he return to go as he came, and shall take nothing of his labour, which he may carry away in his hand...For he cometh in with vanity, and departeth in darkness, and his name shall be covered with darkness. (Eccles. 5:15, 6:4)

Consider all the ancient men of the earth who made great names for themselves and built kingdoms. We know very little about them. They are gone, and their names are covered with darkness. Even the presidents of the United States, all great men of high stature, are quickly forgotten. U.S. citizens trained in history during their school years often cannot name the president in 1835, or 1902, or 1812 from memory. These great men are forgotten.

To begin to understand your need for God, you must understand how small and insignificant you are. Your life is like a vapor.

> Wherefore he saith, God resisteth the proud, but giveth grace unto the humble…For what is your life? It is even a vapour, that appeareth for a little time, and then vanisheth away. (James 4:6, 14)

> The LORD is nigh unto them that are of a broken heart; and saveth such as be of a contrite spirit. (Ps. 34:18)

> The sacrifices of God are a broken spirit: a broken and a contrite heart, O God, thou wilt not despise. (Ps. 51:17)

> For thus saith the high and lofty One that inhabiteth eternity, whose name is Holy; I dwell in the high and holy place, with him also that is of a contrite and humble spirit, to revive the spirit of the humble, and to revive the heart of the contrite ones. (Isa. 57:15)

> For all those things hath mine hand made, and all those things have been, saith the LORD: but to this man will I look, even to him that is poor and of a contrite spirit, and trembleth at my word. (Isa. 66:2)

> Now I Nebuchadnezzar praise and extol and honour the King of heaven, all whose works are truth, and his ways judgment: and those that walk in pride he is able to abase. (Dan. 4:37)

Gird up thy loins now like a man: I will demand of thee, and declare thou unto me. Wilt thou also disannul my judgment? wilt thou condemn me, that thou mayest be righteous? Hast thou an arm like God? or canst thou thunder with a voice like him? (Job 40:7–9)

If you humble yourself before God, he will draw near. And when he draws near, he will begin to open your eyes to who he is, and to his Son, Jesus Christ.

Sinful and Stained

The Bible teaches that none of us can please God with works of righteousness. God is very clear that we cannot earn our way to heaven. When you come to understand your inability to provide your own path to salvation, you will begin to look to God. You will realize that you need a savior.

Not every one that saith unto me, Lord, Lord, shall enter into the kingdom of heaven; but he that doeth the will of my Father which is in heaven. Many will say to me in that day, Lord, Lord, have we not prophesied in thy name? and in thy name have cast out devils? and in thy name done many wonderful works? And then will I profess unto them, I never knew you: depart from me, ye that work iniquity. (Matt. 7:21–23)

All of our combined righteousness is considered stained and filthy rags to God:

As it is written, There is none righteous, no, not one. (Rom. 3:10)

But we are all as an unclean thing, and all our righteousnesses are as filthy rags; and we all do fade as a leaf; and our iniquities, like the wind, have taken us away. (Isa. 64:6)

Jesus, the Only Way to the Father

Only those who do the will of the Father will be recognized by God. And the will of the Father, as the Gospels and epistles make clear, is that we recognize his Son, Jesus Christ, as the only path to the Father and to salvation. God is very clear that without Jesus Christ, there is no access to him. There is only one way.

> Jesus saith unto him, I am the way, the truth, and the life: no man cometh unto the Father, but by me. (John 14:6)

> For there is one God, and one mediator between God and men, the man Christ Jesus. (1 Tim. 2:5)

Faith and Belief in Jesus Christ

In faith—which is simply another word for *trust* or *belief*—we must believe that God the Father has established the one mediator in Jesus Christ. Jesus Christ was sent from God to seek and to save the lost:

> And no man hath ascended up to heaven, but he that came down from heaven, even the Son of man which is in heaven. And as Moses lifted up the serpent in the wilderness, even so must the Son of man be lifted up: that whosoever believeth in him should not perish, but have eternal life. For God so loved the world, that he gave his only begotten Son, that whosoever believeth in him should not perish, but have everlasting life. For God sent not his Son into the world to condemn the world; but that the world through him might be saved. He that believeth on him is not condemned: but he that believeth not is condemned already, because he hath not believed in the name of the only begotten Son of God. (John 3:13–18)

> But without faith it is impossible to please him: for he that cometh to God must believe that he is, and that he is a rewarder of them that diligently seek him. (Heb. 11:6)

For by grace are ye saved through faith; and that not of yourselves: it is the gift of God: not of works, lest any man should boast. (Eph. 2:8–9)

Repentance and Confession of Jesus as Lord

The Bible says that you must call upon the Lord to be saved. At the same time, sincere belief in God leads to repentance. Since we are all filthy sinners, we all need to repent before Almighty God.

> I came not to call the righteous, but sinners to repentance. (Luke 5:32)

> And saying, The time is fulfilled, and the kingdom of God is at hand: repent ye, and believe the gospel. (Mark 1:15)

> I tell you, Nay: but, except ye repent, ye shall all likewise perish. (Luke 13:3)

> And the times of this ignorance God winked at; but now commandeth all men every where to repent. (Acts 17:30)

> That if thou shalt confess with thy mouth the Lord Jesus, and shalt believe in thine heart that God hath raised him from the dead, thou shalt be saved. For with the heart man believeth unto righteousness; and with the mouth confession is made unto salvation. For the scripture saith, Whosoever believeth on him shall not be ashamed. For there is no difference between the Jew and the Greek: for the same Lord over all is rich unto all that call upon him. For whosoever shall call upon the name of the Lord shall be saved. (Rom. 10:9–13)

The Faith Born of Love

We should fear God, but we should also love him. We cannot forget that the offer of salvation which God extends to us came at the cost of his own beloved Son's life. His offer of salvation is open to all men, and he calls all men to humbleness, faith, belief, repentance, and confession of Jesus Christ as Lord and King. The best illustration of the call of God to all men is written in Acts 2, shortly after the resurrection and ascension of Jesus Christ into heaven. The apostle Peter stood up in a large public gathering and explained the way to salvation:

> Ye men of Judaea, and all ye that dwell at Jerusalem, be this known unto you, and hearken to my words: for these are not drunken, as ye suppose, seeing it is but the third hour of the day. But this is that which was spoken by the prophet Joel; And it shall come to pass in the last days, saith God, I will pour out of my Spirit upon all flesh: and your sons and your daughters shall prophesy, and your young men shall see visions, and your old men shall dream dreams: and on my servants and on my handmaidens I will pour out in those days of my Spirit; and they shall prophesy: and I will shew wonders in heaven above, and signs in the earth beneath; blood, and fire, and vapour of smoke: the sun shall be turned into darkness, and the moon into blood, before the great and notable day of the Lord come: *and it shall come to pass, that whosoever shall call on the name of the Lord shall be saved.*
>
> Ye men of Israel, hear these words; Jesus of Nazareth, a man approved of God among you by miracles and wonders and signs, which God did by him in the midst of you, as ye yourselves also know: him, being delivered by the determinate counsel and foreknowledge of God, ye have taken, and by wicked hands have crucified and slain: whom God hath raised up, having loosed the pains of death: because it was not possible that he should be holden of it. For David speaketh concerning him, I foresaw the Lord always before my face, for he is on my right hand, that I should not be moved: therefore did my heart rejoice, and my tongue was glad; moreover also my flesh shall rest in hope: because thou wilt not leave my soul in hell, neither wilt thou suffer thine Holy One to see corruption. Thou hast made known to me *the ways of life;* thou

shalt make me full of joy with thy countenance.

Men and brethren, let me freely speak unto you of the patriarch David, that he is both dead and buried, and his sepulchre is with us unto this day. Therefore being a prophet, and knowing that God had sworn with an oath to him, that of the fruit of his loins, according to the flesh, he would raise up Christ to sit on his throne; he seeing this before spake of the resurrection of Christ, that his soul was not left in hell, neither his flesh did see corruption. This Jesus hath God raised up, whereof we all are witnesses. Therefore being by the right hand of God exalted, and having received of the Father the promise of the Holy Ghost, he hath shed forth this, which ye now see and hear. For David is not ascended into the heavens: but he saith himself, The Lord said unto my Lord, Sit thou on my right hand, until I make thy foes thy footstool.

Therefore let all the house of Israel know assuredly, that God hath made the same Jesus, whom ye have crucified, both Lord and Christ. *Now when they heard this, they were pricked in their heart,* and said unto Peter and to the rest of the apostles, *Men and brethren, what shall we do?*

Then Peter said unto them, *Repent, and be baptized every one of you in the name of Jesus Christ for the remission of sins, and ye shall receive the gift of the Holy Ghost.* For the promise is unto you, and to your children, and to all that are afar off, even as many as the LORD our God shall call. (Acts 2:14–39, emphasis mine)

The Bible records that the crowd was pricked in their hearts. If you are reading this and feeling a similar prick in your heart, know that God is drawing you to himself. Jesus said, "No man can come to me, except the Father which hath sent me draw him: and I will raise him up at the last day" (John 6:44). The prick in the heart is God reaching out to give you the knowledge of salvation (Luke 1:77, "To give knowledge of salvation unto his people by the remission of their sins"). Do not ignore or push away this prick in your heart, for now is the time and now is the day of your salvation.

For he saith, I have heard thee in a time accepted, and in the day of salvation have I succoured thee: behold, now is the accepted time; behold, *now is the day of salvation.* (2 Cor. 6:2, emphasis mine)

The Key to Salvation in Christ

The people listening to Peter asked the question, "What shall we do?" In answer, the key to salvation is found in Acts 2:21 and Acts 2:38:

> And it shall come to pass, that whosoever shall call on the name of the Lord shall be saved…Then Peter said unto them, Repent, and be baptized every one of you in the name of Jesus Christ for the remission of sins, and ye shall receive the gift of the Holy Ghost.

The key is to repent and call out to God in the name of the Lord Jesus Christ for salvation. You put your newfound faith into action by seeking out baptism in obedience to God's command.

True repentance and belief in God will change you. You will develop a desire to know more about him and learn his commandments. You will be drawn by his love to love him in return. If you start seeking him out, you will be changed. I know I was.

> Therefore if any man be in Christ, he is a new creature: old things are passed away; behold, all things are become new. (2 Cor. 5:17)

Many have said that salvation is like getting a new lease on life. Others have said it is like becoming a child again, where all the sins and burdens and regrets that you carry around are erased. For me, salvation was like a conversion. I believed in God, but when I came to understand who he was, then I was changed into one who desired to know more about God and to follow him. My faith turned into action.

God has provided me with a life full of joy and a generally worry-free existence. (I'm not afraid of death or growing old—there's too much to look forward to!) If you will come to the knowledge of salvation in God and acknowledge his control over everything, you can let go of your cares and worries and the things that keep you up at night. The Bible says the path that God prescribes is life. Proverbs 12:28 reads, "In the way of righteousness *is life:* and in the pathway thereof there is no death."

In Christ, I gave up what I thought was a life and instead found a true life. Look at what God promises for you if you follow him. You don't have to wait until the next life and some far-off promise of heaven. The benefits of submitting to Jesus Christ are for today:

> But the fruit of the Spirit is love, joy, peace, longsuffering, gentleness, goodness, faith, meekness, temperance: against such there is no law. (Gal. 5:22–23)

> Take my yoke upon you, and learn of me; for I am meek and lowly in heart: and ye shall find rest unto your souls. For my yoke is easy, and my burden is light. (Matt. 11:29–30)

> It is the spirit that quickeneth; the flesh profiteth nothing: the words that I speak unto you, they are spirit, and they are life… Then Simon Peter answered him, Lord, to whom shall we go? thou hast the words of eternal life. (John 6:63, 68)

> Thou wilt shew me the path of life: in thy presence is fulness of joy; at thy right hand there are pleasures for evermore. (Ps. 16:11)

This is a great bargain! God offers the path of life and fullness of joy. Isn't this what we all crave? We all want love. We all want joy. We all want peace in our lives. God is offering all of this if you will just accept it.

Discovering God and learning more about him through the Bible has enriched my life beyond description. John records this of Jesus: "And there are also many other things which Jesus did, the which, if they should be written every one, I suppose that even the world itself could not contain the books that should be written. Amen" (John 21:25). My life has been filled with the benefits of knowing and serving a true and living God. I'm actually starting to consider that my next book should be about what God has done for me—the direct prayers he has answered and the things he has taught me through his Word. I have more than enough material to fill a volume.

The Choice

Wherever we may be in the chronology of history, this is *your* last generation. You don't have another life to live. Your life will soon be over and quickly forgotten. However, God knows who you are. And God cares for you. Jesus said in Matthew 10:29–32, "Are not two sparrows sold for a farthing? and one of them shall not fall on the ground without your Father. But the very hairs of your head are all numbered. Fear ye not therefore, ye are of more value than many sparrows. Whosoever therefore shall confess me before men, him will I confess also before my Father which is in heaven."

John 3:16 records, "For God so loved the world, that he gave his only begotten Son, that whosoever believeth in him should not perish, but have everlasting life." Jesus Christ provided the ultimate sacrifice by his death on the cross in order that we might gain the salvation of God. He is our Savior, who did for us what we could never do for ourselves. Ephesians 5:1–2 says, "Be ye therefore followers of God, as dear children; and walk in love, as Christ also hath loved us, *and hath given himself for us an offering and a sacrifice to God* for a sweetsmelling savour" (emphasis mine).

Will you believe in God? Will you believe his assurance that the only path to salvation is through Jesus Christ? Will you humble yourself before him? Will you repent? Will you, by faith, seek God, attend church, and learn the Bible so that you can understand what he requires of you? Hebrews 11:6 says that "He is a rewarder of them that diligently seek him."

I pray that you will seek God. Believing in God and accepting Jesus Christ as your Savior is only the first step. Following and obeying him is where the true Christian life begins, when you move past your initial commitment and begin to develop a relationship with God Almighty. If you are a Christian in name but not in lifestyle, then I urge you to begin reading the Bible for yourself. If you stay committed to reading the Word, I guarantee it will change your life and prepare you for the things to come.

Whether your future holds the dreaded experience of the Great Tribulation or the simple and unstoppable age progression toward death, God's Word provides all the comfort and assurances we need to face tomorrow with hope and without fear.

"Let us hear the conclusion of the whole matter: Fear God, and keep his commandments: for this is the whole duty of man." (Eccles. 12:13)

Are you willing to take a fresh look at the Word of God, pray, and seek his counsel in these matters of great consequence?

Index

Summary of The Signs

Below is a summary of the signs given in the Gospels and Revelation, as they are laid out in this book. All emphasis in the quotations is mine.

The First Sign: Deception

Matthew 24:5: "For many shall come in my name, saying, I am Christ; and shall deceive many."

Luke 21:8b: "For many shall come in my name, saying, I am Christ; *and the time draweth near:* go ye not therefore after them."

Mark 13:6: "For many shall come in my name, saying, I am Christ; and shall deceive many."

The Second Sign: Multiple Wars

Matthew 24:6: "And ye shall hear of wars and rumours of wars: see that ye be not troubled: for all these things must come to pass, *but the end is not yet.*"

Luke 21:9: "But when ye shall hear of wars and commotions, be not terrified: for these things *must first* come to pass; but the end is not by and by."

Mark 13:7: "And when ye shall hear of wars and rumours of wars, be ye not troubled: for such things must needs be; but *the end shall not be yet.*"

The Third Sign: The First Four Seals in Revelation and the Beginning of Sorrows

Seal #1: World Leader

Revelation 6:1–2: "And I saw when the Lamb opened one of the seals, and I heard, as it were the noise of thunder, one of the four beasts saying, Come and see. And I saw, and behold a white horse: and he that sat on him had a bow; and a crown was given unto him: and he went forth conquering, and to conquer."

Seal #2: War

Matthew 24:7: "For nation shall rise against nation, and kingdom against kingdom."

Luke 21:10: "Then said he unto them, Nation shall rise against nation, and kingdom against kingdom."

Mark 13:8: "For nation shall rise against nation, and kingdom against kingdom."

Revelation 6:3–4: "And when he had opened the second seal, I heard the second beast say, Come and see. And there went out another horse that was red: and power was given to him that sat thereon to take peace from the earth, and that they should kill one another: and there was given unto him a great sword."

Seal #3: Famine

Matthew 24:7: "And there shall be famines."

Luke 21:10: "And famines . . ."

Mark 31:8: "And there shall be famines and troubles."

Revelation 6:5–6: "And when he had opened the third seal, I heard the third beast say, Come and see. And I beheld, and lo a black horse; and he that sat on him had a pair of balances in his hand. And I heard a voice in the midst of the four beasts say, A measure of wheat for a penny, and three measures of barley for a penny; and see thou hurt not the oil and the wine."

Seal #4: Pestilence

Matthew 24:7: "And pestilences…"

Luke 21:10: "And pestilences…"

Revelation 6:7–8: "And when he had opened the fourth seal, I heard the voice of the fourth beast say, Come and see. And I looked, and behold a pale horse: and his name that sat on him was Death, and Hell followed with him. And power was given unto them over the fourth part of the earth, to kill with sword, and with hunger, and with death, and with the beasts of the earth."

Matthew 24:7: "And earthquakes, in divers places."

Luke 21:11: "And great earthquakes shall be in divers places."

Mark 31:8: "And there shall be earthquakes in divers places."

Matthew 24:8: "All these are the beginning of sorrows."

Mark 31:8: "These are the beginnings of sorrows."

The Fourth Sign: The Worldwide Gospel Witness and the Seal of God on the 144,000

Matthew 24:14: "And this gospel of the kingdom shall be preached in all the world for a witness unto all nations; *and then* shall the end come."

Mark 13:10: "And the gospel *must first* be published among all nations."

Revelation 7:1–4: "And after these things I saw four angels standing on the four corners of the earth, holding the four winds of the earth, that the wind should not blow on the earth, nor on the sea, nor on any tree. And I saw another angel ascending from the east, having the seal of the living God: and he cried with a loud voice to the four angels, to whom it was given to hurt the earth and the sea, saying, Hurt not the earth, neither the sea, nor the trees, till we have sealed the servants of our God in their foreheads. And I heard the number of them which were sealed: and there were sealed an hundred and forty and four thousand of all the tribes of the children of Israel."

The Fifth Sign: Persecution

Seal #5: Martyred Souls Under the Altar

Matthew 24:9–13: *"Then* shall they deliver you up to be afflicted, and shall kill you: and ye shall be hated of all nations for my name's sake. And then shall many be offended, and shall betray one another, and shall hate one another. And many false prophets shall rise, and shall deceive many. And because iniquity shall abound, the love of many shall wax cold. But he that shall endure unto the end, the same shall be saved."

Luke 21:12–19: "But *before all these* [i.e. before Luke 11b, which details the fearful sights and great signs from heaven which are the same as the sixth seal in the Revelation], they shall lay their hands on you, and persecute you, delivering you up to the synagogues, and into prisons, being brought before kings and rulers for my name's sake. And it shall turn to you for a testimony. Settle it therefore in your hearts, not to meditate before what ye shall answer: for I will give you a mouth and wisdom, which all your adversaries shall not be able to gainsay nor resist. And ye shall be betrayed both by parents, and brethren, and kinsfolks, and friends; and some of you shall they cause to be put to death. And ye shall be hated of all men for my name's sake. But there shall not an hair of your head perish. In your patience possess ye your souls."

Mark 13:9: "But take heed to yourselves: for they shall deliver you up to councils; and in the synagogues ye shall be beaten: and ye shall be brought before rulers and kings for my sake, for a testimony against them."

Mark 13:11–13: "But when they shall lead you, and deliver you up, take no thought beforehand what ye shall speak, neither do ye premeditate: but whatsoever shall be given you in that hour, that speak ye: for it is not ye that speak, but the Holy Ghost. Now the brother shall betray the brother to death, and the father the son; and children shall rise up against their parents, and shall cause them to be put to death. And ye shall be hated of all men for my name's sake: but he that shall endure unto the end, the same shall be saved."

Revelation 13:1–18: "And I stood upon the sand of the sea, and saw a beast rise up out of the sea, having seven heads and ten horns, and upon his horns ten crowns, and upon his heads the name of blasphemy. And the beast which I saw was like unto a leopard, and his feet were as the feet of a bear, and his mouth as the mouth of a lion: and the dragon gave him his power, and his seat, and great authority. And I saw one of his heads as it were wounded to death; and his deadly wound was healed: and all the world wondered after the beast. And they worshipped the dragon which gave power unto the beast: and they worshipped the beast, saying, Who is like unto the beast? who is able to make war with him? And there was given unto him a mouth speaking great things and blasphemies; and power was given unto him to continue forty and two months. And he opened his mouth in blasphemy against God, to blaspheme his name, and his tabernacle, and them that dwell in heaven. *And it was given unto him to make war with the saints, and to overcome them: and power was given him over all kindreds, and tongues, and nations.* And all that dwell upon the earth shall worship him, whose names are not written in the book of life of the Lamb slain from the foundation of the world. If any man have an ear, let him hear. He that leadeth into captivity shall go into captivity: he that killeth with the sword must be killed with the sword. Here is the patience and the faith of the saints. And I beheld another beast coming up out of the earth; and he had two horns like a lamb, and he spake as a dragon. And he exerciseth all the power of the first beast before him, and causeth the earth and them which dwell therein to worship the first beast, whose deadly wound was healed. And he doeth great wonders, so that he maketh fire come down from heaven on the earth in the sight of men, and deceiveth them that dwell on the earth by the means of those miracles which he had power to do in the sight of the beast; saying to them that dwell on the earth, that they should make an image to the beast, which had the wound by a sword, and did live. And he had power to give life unto the image of the beast, that the image of the beast should both speak, and cause that as many as would not worship the image of the beast should be killed. And he causeth all, both small and great, rich and poor, free and bond, to receive a mark in their right hand, or in their foreheads: and that no man might buy or sell, save he that had the mark, or the name of the beast, or the number of his name. Here is wisdom. Let him that hath understanding count the number of the beast: for it is the number of a man; and his number is Six hundred threescore and six."

Revelation 6:9–11: "And when he had opened the fifth seal, I saw under the altar the souls of them that were slain for the word of God, and for the testimony which they held: and they cried with a loud voice, saying, How long, O Lord, holy and true, dost thou not judge and avenge our blood on them that dwell on the earth? And white robes were given unto every one of them; and it was said unto them, that they should *rest* yet for a little season, until their fellowservants also and their brethren, that should be killed as they were, should be fulfilled."

Revelation 14:12–13: "Here is the patience of the saints: here are they that keep the commandments of God, and the faith of Jesus. And I heard a voice from heaven saying unto me, Write, Blessed are the dead which die in the Lord from henceforth: Yea, saith the Spirit, that they may rest from their labours; and their works do follow them."

Daniel 7:21: "I beheld, and the same horn made *war with the saints,* and *prevailed against them.*"

The Sixth Sign: The Abomination of Desolation

Matthew 24:15–20: *"When* ye therefore shall see the abomination of desolation, spoken of by Daniel the prophet, stand in the holy place, (whoso readeth, let him understand:) then let them which be in Judaea flee into the mountains: let him which is on the housetop not come down to take any thing out of his house: neither let him which is in the field return back to take his clothes. And woe unto them that are with child, and to them that give suck in those days! But pray ye that your flight be not in the winter, neither on the sabbath day."

Luke 21:20–24: "And *when* ye shall see Jerusalem compassed with armies, then know that the desolation thereof is nigh. Then let them which are in Judaea flee to the mountains; and let them which are in the midst of it depart out; and let not them that are in the countries enter thereinto. For these be the days of vengeance, that all things which are written may be fulfilled. But woe unto them that are with child, and to them that give suck, in those days! for there shall be great distress in the land, and wrath upon this people. And they shall fall by the edge of the sword, and shall be led away captive into all nations: and Jerusalem shall be trodden down of the Gentiles, until the times of the Gentiles be fulfilled."

Mark 13:14–18: "But *when* ye shall see the abomination of desolation, spoken of by Daniel the prophet, standing where it ought not, (let him that readeth understand,) then let them that be in Judaea flee to the mountains: and let him that is on the housetop not go down into the house, neither enter therein, to take any thing out of his house: and let him that is in the field not turn back again for to take up his garment. But woe to them that are with child, and to them that give suck in those days! And pray ye that your flight be not in the winter."

Daniel 9:27: "And he shall confirm the covenant with many for one week: and in the midst of the week he shall cause the sacrifice and the oblation to cease, and for the overspreading of abominations he shall make it desolate, even until the consummation, and that determined shall be poured upon the desolate."

Revelation 13:3–4: "And I saw one of his heads as it were wounded to death; and his deadly wound was healed: and all the world wondered after the beast. And they worshipped the dragon which gave power unto the beast: and they worshipped the beast, saying, Who is like unto the beast? who is able to make war with him?"

2 Thessalonians 2:1–5: "Now we beseech you, brethren, by the coming of our Lord Jesus Christ, and by our gathering together unto him, that ye be not soon shaken in mind, or be troubled, neither by spirit, nor by word, nor by letter as from us, as that the day of Christ is at hand. Let no man deceive you by any means: for that day *shall not come,* except there come a falling away *first,* and that man of sin be revealed, the son of perdition; who opposeth and exalteth himself above all that is called God, or that is worshipped; so that he as God sitteth in the temple of God, shewing himself that he is God. Remember ye not, that, when I was yet with you, I told you these things?"

The Seventh Sign: Great Tribulation

Seal #6: Great Tribulation

Matthew 24:21–22: *"For then* shall be *great tribulation,* such as was not since the beginning of the world to this time, no, nor ever shall be. And except those days should be shortened, there should no flesh be saved: but for the elect's sake those days shall be shortened."

Luke 21:11b: "And fearful sights and great signs shall there be from heaven."

Luke 21:25–26: *"And* there shall be signs in the sun, and in the moon, and in the stars; and upon the earth distress of nations, with perplexity; the sea and the waves roaring; men's hearts failing them for fear, and for looking after those things which are coming on the earth: for the powers of heaven shall be shaken."

Mark 13:19: *"For in those days* shall be *affliction,* such as was not from the beginning of the creation which God created unto this time, neither shall be. And except that the Lord had shortened those days, no flesh should be saved: but for the elect's sake, whom he hath chosen, he hath shortened the days."

Revelation 6:12–17: "And I beheld when he had opened the sixth seal, and, lo, there was a great earthquake; and the sun became black as sackcloth of hair, and the moon became as blood; and the stars of heaven fell unto the earth, even as a fig tree casteth her untimely figs, when she is shaken of a mighty wind. And the heaven departed as a scroll when it is rolled together; and every mountain and island were moved out of their places. And the kings of the earth, and the great men, and the rich men, and the chief captains, and the mighty men, and every bondman, and every free man, hid themselves in the dens and in the rocks of the mountains; and said to the mountains and rocks, Fall on us, and hide us from the face of him that sitteth on the throne, and from the wrath of the Lamb: for the great day of his wrath is come; and who shall be able to stand?"

Revelation 7:9–17: "After this I beheld, and, lo, a great multitude, which no man could number, of all nations, and kindreds, and people, and tongues, stood before the throne, and before the Lamb, clothed with white robes, and palms in their hands; and cried with a loud voice, saying, Salvation to our God which sitteth upon the throne, and unto the Lamb. And all the angels stood round about the throne, and about the elders and the four beasts, and fell before the throne on their faces, and worshipped God, saying, Amen: Blessing, and glory, and wisdom, and thanksgiving, and honour, and power, and might, be unto our God for ever and ever. Amen. And one of the elders answered, saying unto me, *What are these which are arrayed in white robes? and whence came they?* And I said unto him, Sir, thou knowest. And he said to me, *These are they which came out of great tribulation,* and have washed their robes, and made them white in the blood of the Lamb. Therefore are they before the throne of God, and serve him day and night in his temple: and he that sitteth on the throne shall dwell among them. They shall hunger no more, neither thirst any more; neither shall the sun light on them, nor any heat. For the Lamb which is in the midst of the throne shall feed them, and shall lead them unto living fountains of waters: and God shall wipe away all tears from their eyes."

LUKE	THE SIXTH SEAL IN REVELATION
Great Signs in Heaven…	
Signs in Sun	The sun became black as sackcloth of hair
Signs in Moon	The moon became blood
Signs in the Stars	The stars of heaven fall to the earth
Distress and Perplexity of Nations	The kings of the earth (nations) are distressed
Men's Hearts Failing from Fear	Men hide themselves for fear and ask the mountains and rocks to fall on them to hide them from the face of him that sitteth on the throne and from the wrath of the Lamb
Sea and Waves Roaring	A great earthquake where every mountain and island is moved out of its place. The natural result would be multiple tsunamis.
The Powers of Heaven Shaken	The heaven departed as a scroll when it is rolled together

THE EIGHTH SIGN: FALSE CHRISTS AND FALSE PROPHETS

Matthew 24:23–26: "Then if any man shall say unto you, Lo, here is Christ, or there; believe it not. For there shall arise false Christs, and false prophets, and shall shew great signs and wonders; insomuch that, if it were possible, they shall *deceive the very elect*. Behold, I have told you before. Wherefore if they shall say unto you, Behold, he is in the desert; go not forth: behold, he is in the secret chambers; believe it not."

Mark 13:21–23: "And then if any man shall say to you, Lo, here is Christ; or, lo, he is there; *believe him not:* for false Christs and false prophets shall rise, and shall shew signs and wonders, to seduce, if it were possible, even the elect. But take ye heed: behold, *I have foretold you all things."*

Revelation 13:11–15: "And I beheld another beast coming up out of the earth; and he had two horns like a lamb, and he spake as a dragon. And he exerciseth all the power of the first beast before him, and causeth the earth and them which dwell therein to worship the first beast, whose deadly wound was healed. And he doeth great wonders, so that he maketh fire come down from heaven on the earth in the sight of men, and deceiveth them that dwell on the earth by the means of those miracles which he had power to do in the sight of the beast; saying to them that dwell on the earth, that they should make an image to the beast, which had the wound by a sword, and did live. And he had power to give life unto the image of the beast, that the image of the beast should both speak, and cause that as many as would not worship the image of the beast should be killed."

The Ninth Sign: Heaven and Earth Shaken—Again; The Trumpets of Revelation

Matthew 24:29: "Immediately *after* the tribulation of those days shall the sun be darkened, and the moon shall not give her light, and the stars shall fall from heaven, and the powers of the heavens shall be shaken."

Mark 13:24–25: "But in those days, after that tribulation, the sun shall be darkened, and the moon shall not give her light, and the stars of heaven shall fall, and the powers that are in heaven shall be shaken."

Revelation 8:7–13: "The first angel sounded, and there followed hail and fire mingled with blood, and they were cast upon the earth: and the third part of trees was burnt up, and all green grass was burnt up. And the second angel sounded, and as it were a great mountain burning with fire was cast into the sea: and the third part of the sea became blood; and the third part of the creatures which were in the sea, and had life, died; and the third part of the ships were destroyed. And the third angel sounded, and there fell a great star from heaven, burning as it were a lamp, and it fell upon the third part of the rivers, and upon the fountains of waters; and the name of the star is called Wormwood: and the third part of the waters became wormwood; and many men died of the waters, because they were made bitter. And the fourth angel sounded, and the third part of the sun was smitten, and the third part of the moon, and the third part of the stars; so as the third part of them was darkened, and the day shone not for a third part of it, and the night likewise. And I beheld, and heard an angel flying through the midst of heaven, saying with a loud voice, Woe, woe, woe, to the inhabiters of the earth by reason of the other voices of the trumpet of the three angels, which are yet to sound!"

Revelation 9:1–6: "And the fifth angel sounded, and I saw a star fall from heaven unto the earth: and to him was given the key of the bottomless pit. And he opened the bottomless pit; and there arose a smoke out of the pit, as the smoke of a great furnace; and the sun and the air were darkened by reason of the smoke of the pit. And there came out of the smoke locusts upon the earth: and unto them was given power, as the scorpions of the earth have power. And it was commanded them that they should not hurt the grass of the earth, neither any green thing, neither any tree; but *only those men* which have *not the seal of God* in their foreheads. And to them it was given that they should not kill them, but that they should be tormented five months: and their torment was as the torment of a scorpion, when he striketh a man. And in those days shall men seek death, and shall not find it; and shall desire to die, and death shall flee from them."

MATTHEW AND MARK

Ninth Sign: Revelation Trumpets

Gospels = Powers of heaven shaken
1st Trumpet = Hail, Fire, Blood, 1/3 of the trees/grass burn away
2nd Trumpet = Burning mountain, 1/3 of the sea becomes blood

Gospels = Stars fall from heaven
3rd Trumpet = Star from heaven, 1/3 of the waters become bitter

Gospels = Sun darkened
4th Trumpet = 1/3 of the sun darkened

Gospels = Moon darkened

4th Trumpet = 1/3 of the moon darkened
5th Trumpet = Demonic torment of men

The Tenth Sign: The Return of Christ at the Rapture; The Beginning of the Sound of the Seventh Trumpet

Matthew 24:27–31: "For as the lightning cometh out of the east, and shineth even unto the west; so shall also the coming of the Son of man be. For wheresoever the carcase is, there will the eagles be gathered together. *And then* shall appear the sign of the Son of man in heaven: and then shall all the tribes of the earth mourn, and they shall see the Son of man coming in the clouds of heaven with power and great glory. And he shall send his angels with a great sound of a trumpet, and they shall gather together his elect from the four winds, from one end of heaven to the other."

Luke 21:27–28: *"And then* shall they see the Son of man coming in a cloud with power and great glory. And when these things begin to come to pass, then look up, and lift up your heads; for your redemption draweth nigh."

Luke 17:24: "For as the lightning, that lighteneth out of the one part under heaven, shineth unto the other part under heaven; so shall also the Son of man be in his day."

Mark 13:26–27: *"And then* shall they see the Son of man coming in the clouds with great power and glory. *And then* shall he send his angels, and shall gather together his elect from the four winds, from the uttermost part of the earth to the uttermost part of heaven."

2 Thessalonians 2:1: "Now we beseech you, brethren, by the coming of our Lord Jesus Christ, and by our gathering together unto him."

1 Thessalonians 4:16–18: "For the Lord himself shall descend from heaven with a shout, with the *voice* of the archangel, and with the trump of God: and the dead in Christ shall rise first: then we which are alive and remain shall be caught up together with them in the clouds, to meet the Lord in

the air: and so shall we ever be with the Lord. Wherefore comfort one another with these words."

Revelation 1:7: "Behold, he cometh with clouds; and every eye shall see him, and they also which pierced him: and all kindreds of the earth shall wail because of him. Even so, Amen."

1 Corinthians 15:51–52: "Behold, I shew you a *mystery;* we shall not all sleep, but we shall all be changed, in a moment, in the twinkling of an eye, at the *last trump:* for the trumpet shall sound, and the dead shall be raised incorruptible, and we shall be changed."

Revelation 10:7: "But in the days of the *voice* of the seventh angel, when he shall *begin to sound,* the *mystery* of God should be finished, as he hath declared to his servants the prophets."

Endnotes

1. George Müller, *A Narrative of Some of the Lord's Dealings with George Müller*, Volume 1 (Spring Lake, MI: Dust & Ashes Publications, 2003), 39–40.
2. Marvin Rosenthal, *The Pre-Wrath Rapture of the Church* (Nashville: Thomas Nelson, 1990), 53–54.
3. For more on Irving's life see Arnold Dallimore, *The Life of Edward Irving: The Forerunner of the Charismatic Movement* (Edinburgh: Banner of Truth, 1983) and Gordon Strachan, *The Pentecostal Theology of Edward Irving* (Peabody, MA: Hendrickson Publishers, 1988).
4. Edward Irving, *The Last Days: A Discourse on the Evil Character of These Our Times, Proving Them to be The 'Perilous Times' and the 'Last Days'* (London: James Nisbit, 1850), 10–22.
5. John H. Gerstner, *Wrongly Dividing the Word of Truth* (Brentwood, TN: Wolgemuth & Hyatt, 1991), 25.
6. Sandy Fiedler, "How Did We Get the Idea of the Pre-Trib Rapture?", *Studies in Reformed Theology*, Issue 06, http://www.reformedtheology.org/html/issue06/pre-trib.htm.
7. Ibid.
8. Sandy Fiedler, "How Did We Get the Idea of the Pre-Trib Rapture?", *Studies in Reformed Theology*, Issue 06, http://www.reformedtheology.org/html/issue06/pre-trib.htm.
9. A list of separate messiah claims can be found at http://en.wikipedia.org/wiki/List_of_messiah_claimants.
10. "Crowd Packs Amphitheater for Man Claiming He's Jesus Christ Reincarnated," *Internet Broadcasting Systems* and *Local6.com,* Orlando, FL, May 6, 2007.
11. "The World At War," *Global Security.org,* http://www.globalsecurity.org/military/world/war/.
12. Kathryn Hadley, "Alarming increase in wars," *History Today,* July 12, 2011, http://www.historytoday.com/blog/2011/07/alarming-increase-wars.

13. Robert Bruce Fruehling, *The Revelation of King Arthur* (Enumclaw, WA: Winepress Publishing, 2010), 19
14. Robert Bruce Fruehling, *The Revelation of King Arthur* (Enumclaw, WA: Winepress Publishing, 2010), 19
15. Martin Luther, *On the Jews and Their Lies, 1543,* transl. by Martin H. Bertram, http://www.humanitas-international.org/showcase/chronography/documents/luther-jews.htm.
16. Eric Metaxas, *Bonhoeffer: Pastor, Martyr, Prophet, Spy* (Nashville, TN: Thomas Nelson, 2011), 150–151.
17. Ibid. 150–151.
18. "Antisemitism: The Longest Hatred," *United States Holocaust Memorial Museum,* http://www.ushmm.org/museum/exhibit/focus/antisemitism/.
19. Jim Kouri, "Black Panthers Gearing Up for 'National Day of Action,'" April 22, 2011, *Examiner.com,* http://www.examiner.com/law-enforcement-in-national/black-panthers-gearing-up-for-national-day-of-action.
20. Associated Press, "Dutch Jews want fast punishment for anti-Semitism," February 2, 2011, *FoxNews.com,* http://www.foxnews.com/world/2011/02/02/dutch-jews-want-fast-punishment-anti-semitism/.
21. Alan Buis, "Japan Quake May Have Shortened Earth Days, Movex Axis," March 14, 2011, *NASA,* http://www.nasa.gov/topics/earth/features/japanquake/earth20110314.html.
22. "World Population Prospects, the 2010 Revision: Population," updated June 28, 2011, *United Nations, Department of Economic and Social Affairs,* http://esa.un.org/unpd/wpp/Excel-Data/population.htm.
23. Ibid.
24. "World Population Prospects, the 2010 Revision: Fertility," updated June 28, 2011, *United Nations, Department of Economic and Social Affairs,* http://esa.un.org/unpd/wpp/Excel-Data/fertility.htm.